P9-DDW-357

Liberalism

by

L. T. Hobhouse

The Echo Library 2009

Published by

The Echo Library

Echo Library
131 High St.
Teddington
Middlesex TW11 8HH

www.echo-library.com

Please report serious faults in the text to complaints@echo-library.com

ISBN 978-1-40685-057-4

THE HOME UNIVERSITY LIBRARY

OF MODERN KNOWLEDGE

XXI LIBERALISM

EDITORS OF
THE HOME UNIVERSITY LIBRARY OF MODERN KNOWLEDGE

PROFESSOR GILBERT MURRAY, O.M., LL.D., F.B.A.
PROFESSOR G. N. CLARK, LL.D., F.B.A.
SIR HENRY TIZARD, K.C.B., F.R.S.

4

LIBERALISM

By

L. T. HOBHOUSE

OXFORD UNIVERSITY PRESS
LONDON NEW YORK TORONTO
First published in 1911, and reprinted in 1919, 1923, 1927, 1929, 1934, 1942 and 1944

PRINTED IN GREAT BRITAIN

CONTENTS

LIBERALISM

CHAPTER I

BEFORE LIBERALISM

The modern State is the distinctive product of a unique civilization. But it is a product which is still in the making, and a part of the process is a struggle between new and old principles of social order. To understand the new, which is our main purpose, we must first cast a glance at the old. We must understand what the social structure was, which—mainly, as I shall show, under the inspiration of Liberal ideas—is slowly but surely giving place to the new fabric of the civic State. The older structure itself was by no means primitive. What is truly primitive is very hard to say. But one thing is pretty clear. At all times men have lived in societies, and ties of kinship and of simple neighbourhood underlie every form of social organization. In the simplest societies it seems probable that these ties—reinforced and extended, perhaps, by religious or other beliefs—are the only ones that seriously count. It is certain that of the warp of descent and the woof of intermarriage there is woven a tissue out of which small and rude but close and compact communities are formed. But the ties of kinship and neighbourhood are effective only within narrow limits. While the local group, the clan, or the village community are often the centres of vigorous life, the larger aggregate of the Tribe seldom attains true social and political unity unless it rests upon a military organization. But military organization may serve not only to hold one tribe together but also to hold other tribes in subjection, and thereby, at the cost of much that is most valuable in primitive life, to establish a larger and at the same time a more orderly society. Such an order once established does not, indeed, rest on naked force. The rulers become invested with a sacrosanct authority. It may be that they are gods or descendants of gods. It may be that they are blessed and upheld by an independent priesthood. In either case the powers that be extend their sway not merely over the bodies but over the minds of men. They are ordained of God because they arrange the ordination. Such a government is not necessarily abhorrent to the people nor indifferent to them. But it is essentially government from above. So far as it affects the life of the people at all, it does so by imposing on them duties, as of military service, tribute, ordinances, and even new laws, in such wise and on such principles as seem good to itself. It is not true, as a certain school of jurisprudence held, that law is, as such, a command imposed by a superior upon an inferior, and backed by the sanctions of punishment. But though this is not true of law in general it is a roughly true description of law in that particular stage of society which we may conveniently describe as the Authoritarian.

Now, in the greater part of the world and throughout the greater part of history the two forms of social organization that have been distinguished are the only forms to be found. Of course, they themselves admit of every possible variation of detail, but looking below these variations we find the two recurrent types. On the one hand, there are the small kinship groups, often vigorous enough in themselves, but feeble for purposes of united action. On the other hand, there are larger societies varying in extent and in degree of civilization from a petty negro kingdom to the Chinese Empire, resting on a certain union of military force and religious or quasi-religious belief which, to select a neutral name, we have called the principle of Authority. In the lower stages of civilization there appears, as a rule, to be only one method of suppressing the strife of hostile clans, maintaining the frontier against a common enemy, or establishing the elements of outward order. The alternative to authoritarian rule is relapse into the comparative anarchy of savage life.

But another method made its appearance in classical antiquity. The city state of ancient Greece and Italy was a new type of social organization. It differed from the clan and the commune in several ways. In the first place it contained many clans and villages, and perhaps owed its origin to the coming together of separate clans on the basis not of conquest but of comparatively equal alliance. Though very small as compared with an ancient empire or a modern state it was much larger than a primitive kindred. Its life was more varied and complex. It allowed more free play to the individual, and, indeed, as it developed, it suppressed the old clan organization and substituted new divisions, geographical or other. It was based, in fact, not on kinship as such, but on civic right, and this it was which distinguished it not only from the commune, but from the Oriental monarchy. The law which it recognized and by which it lived was not a command imposed by a superior government on a subject mass. On the contrary, government was itself subject to law, and law was the life of the state, willingly supported by the entire body of free citizens. In this sense the city state was a community of free men. Considered collectively its citizens owned no master. They governed themselves, subject only to principles and rules of life descending from antiquity and owing their force to the spontaneous allegiance of successive generations. In such a community some of the problems that vex us most presented themselves in a very simple form. In particular the relation of the individual to the community was close, direct, and natural. Their interests were obviously bound up together. Unless each man did his duty the State might easily be destroyed and the population enslaved. Unless the State took thought for its citizens it might easily decay. What was still more important, there was no opposition of church and state, no fissure between political and religious life, between the claims of the secular and the spiritual, to distract the allegiance of the citizens, and to set the authority of conscience against the duties of patriotism. It was no feat of the philosophical imagination, but a quite simple and natural expression of the facts to describe such a community as an association of men for the purpose of living well. Ideals to which we win our way back with difficulty and doubt arose naturally out of the conditions of life in ancient Greece.

On the other hand, this simple harmony had very serious limitations, which in the end involved the downfall of the city system. The responsibilities and privileges of the associated life were based not on the rights of human personality but on the rights of citizenship, and citizenship was never co-extensive with the community. The population included slaves or serfs, and in many cities there were large classes descended from the original conquered population, personally free but excluded from the governing circle. Notwithstanding the relative simplicity of social conditions the city was constantly torn by the disputes of faction—in part probably a legacy from the old clan organization, in part a consequence of the growth of wealth and the newer distinction of classes. The evil of faction was aggravated by the ill-success of the city organization in dealing with the problem of inter-state relations. The Greek city clung to its autonomy, and though the principle of federalism which might have solved the problem was ultimately brought into play, it came too late in Greek history to save the nation.

The constructive genius of Rome devised a different method of dealing with the political problems involved in expanding relations. Roman citizenship was extended till it included all Italy and, later on, till it comprised the whole free population of the Mediterranean basin. But this extension was even more fatal to the free self-government of a city state. The population of Italy could not meet in the Forum of Rome or the Plain of Mars to elect consuls and pass laws, and the more wisely it was extended the less valuable for any political purpose did citizenship become. The history of Rome, in fact, might be taken as a vast illustration of the difficulty of building up an extended empire on any basis but that of personal despotism resting on military force and maintaining peace and order through the efficiency of the bureaucratic machine. In this vast mechanism it was the army that was the seat of power, or rather it was each army at its post on some distant frontier that was a potential seat of power. The "secret of the empire" that was early divulged was that an emperor could be made elsewhere than at Rome, and though a certain sanctity remained to the person of the emperor, and legists cherished a dim remembrance of the theory that he embodied the popular will, the fact was that he was the choice of a powerful army, ratified by the God of Battles, and maintaining his power as long as he could suppress any rival pretender. The break-up of the Empire through the continual repetition of military strife was accelerated, not caused, by the presence of barbarism both within and without the frontiers. To restore the elements of order a compromise between central and local jurisdictions was necessary, and the vassal became a local prince owning an allegiance, more or less real as the case might be, to a distant sovereign. Meanwhile, with the prevailing disorder the mass of the population in Western Europe lost its freedom, partly through conquest, partly through the necessity of finding a protector in troublous times. The social structure of the Middle Ages accordingly assumed the hierarchical form which we speak of as the Feudal system. In this thorough-going application of the principle of authority every man, in theory, had his master. The serf held of his lord, who held of a great seigneur, who held of the king. The king in the completer theory held of the emperor who was crowned by the Pope, who held of St. Peter. The chain of descent was complete from the Ruler of the universe to the humblest of the serfs.[1] But within this order the growth of industry and commerce raised up new centres of freedom. The towns in which men were learning anew the lessons of association for united defence and the regulation of common interests, obtained charters of rights from seigneur or king, and on the Continent even succeeded in establishing complete independence. Even in England, where from the Conquest the central power was at its strongest, the corporate towns became for many purposes self-governing communities. The city state was born again, and with it came an outburst of activity, the revival of literature and the arts, the rediscovery of ancient learning, the rebirth of philosophy and science.

The mediæval city state was superior to the ancient in that slavery was no essential element in its existence. On the contrary, by welcoming the fugitive serf and vindicating his freedom it contributed powerfully to the decline of the milder form of servitude. But like the ancient state it was seriously and permanently weakened by internal faction, and like the ancient state it rested the privileges of its members not on the rights of human personality, but on the responsibilities of citizenship. It knew not so much liberty as "liberties," rights of corporations secured by charter, its own rights as a whole secured against king or feudatory and the rest of the world, rights of gilds and crafts within it, and to men or women only as they were members of such bodies. But the real weakness of the city state was once more its isolation. It was but an islet of relative freedom on, or actually within, the borders of a feudal society which grew more powerful with the generations. With the improvement of communications and of the arts of life, the central power, particularly in France and England, began to gain upon its vassals. Feudal disobedience and disorder were suppressed, and by the end of the fifteenth century great unified states, the foundation of modern nations, were already in being. Their emergence involved the widening and in some respects the improvement of the social order; and in its earlier stages it favoured civic autonomy by suppressing local anarchy and feudal privilege. But the growth of centralization was in the end incompatible with the genius of civic independence, and perilous to such elements of political right as had been gained for the population in general as the result of earlier conflicts between the crown and its vassals.

We enter on the modern period, accordingly, with society constituted on a thoroughly authoritarian basis, the kingly power supreme and tending towards arbitrary despotism, and below the king the social hierarchy extending from the great territorial lord to the day-labourer. There is one point gained as compared to earlier forms of society. The base of the pyramid is a class which at least enjoys personal freedom. Serfdom has virtually disappeared in England, and in

---

[1] This is, of course, only one side of mediæval theory, but it is the side which lay nearest to the facts. The reverse view, which derives the authority of government from the governed, made its appearance in the Middle Ages partly under the influence of classical tradition. But its main interest and importance is that it served as a starting-point for the thought of a later time. On the whole subject the reader may consult Gierke, *Political Theories of the Middle Age*, translated by Maitland (Cambridge University Press).

the greater part of France has either vanished or become attenuated to certain obnoxious incidents of the tenure of land. On the other hand, the divorce of the English peasant from the soil has begun, and has laid the foundation of the future social problem as it is to appear in this country.

The modern State accordingly starts from the basis of an authoritarian order, and the protest against that order, a protest religious, political, economic, social, and ethical, is the historic beginning of Liberalism. Thus Liberalism appears at first as a criticism, sometimes even as a destructive and revolutionary criticism. Its negative aspect is for centuries foremost. Its business seems to be not so much to build up as to pull down, to remove obstacles which block human progress, rather than to point the positive goal of endeavour or fashion the fabric of civilization. It finds humanity oppressed, and would set it free. It finds a people groaning under arbitrary rule, a nation in bondage to a conquering race, industrial enterprise obstructed by social privileges or crippled by taxation, and it offers relief. Everywhere it is removing superincumbent weights, knocking off fetters, clearing away obstructions. Is it doing as much for the reconstruction that will be necessary when the demolition is complete? Is Liberalism at bottom a constructive or only a destructive principle? Is it of permanent significance? Does it express some vital truth of social life as such, or is it a temporary phenomenon called forth by the special circumstances of Western Europe, and is its work already so far complete that it can be content to hand on the torch to a newer and more constructive principle, retiring for its own part from the race, or perchance seeking more backward lands for missionary work? These are among the questions that we shall have to answer. We note, for the moment, that the circumstances of its origin suffice to explain the predominance of critical and destructive work without therefrom inferring the lack of ultimate reconstructive power. In point of fact, whether by the aid of Liberalism or through the conservative instincts of the race, the work of reconstruction has gone on side by side with that of demolition, and becomes more important generation by generation. The modern State, as I shall show, goes far towards incorporating the elements of Liberal principle, and when we have seen what these are, and to what extent they are actually realized, we shall be in a better position to understand the essentials of Liberalism, and to determine the question of its permanent value.

CHAPTER II

THE ELEMENTS OF LIBERALISM

I cannot here attempt so much as a sketch of the historical progress of the Liberalizing movement. I would call attention only to the main points at which it assailed the old order, and to the fundamental ideas directing its advance.

1. *Civil Liberty*.

Both logically and historically the first point of attack is arbitrary government, and the first liberty to be secured is the right to be dealt with in accordance with law. A man who has no legal rights against another, but stands entirely at his disposal, to be treated according to his caprice, is a slave to that other. He is "rightless," devoid of rights. Now, in some barbaric monarchies the system of rightlessness has at times been consistently carried through in the relations of subjects to the king. Here men and women, though enjoying customary rights of person and property as against one another, have no rights at all as against the king's pleasure. No European monarch or seignior has ever admittedly enjoyed power of this kind, but European governments have at various times and in various directions exercised or claimed powers no less arbitrary in principle. Thus, by the side of the regular courts of law which prescribe specific penalties for defined offences proved against a man by a regular form of trial, arbitrary governments resort to various extrajudicial forms of arrest, detention, and punishment, depending on their own will and pleasure. Of such a character is punishment by "administrative" process in Russia at the present day; imprisonment by *lettre de cachet* in France under the *ancien régime*; all executions by so-called martial law in times of rebellion, and the suspension of various ordinary guarantees of immediate and fair trial in Ireland. Arbitrary government in this form was one of the first objects of attack by the English Parliament in the seventeenth century, and this first liberty of the subject was vindicated by the Petition of Right, and again by the Habeas Corpus Act. It is significant of much that this first step in liberty should be in reality nothing more nor less than a demand for law. "Freedom of men under government," says Locke, summing up one whole chapter of seventeenth-century controversy, "is to have a standing rule to live by, common to every one of that society and made by the legislative power erected in it."

The first condition of universal freedom, that is to say, is a measure of universal restraint. Without such restraint some men may be free but others will be unfree. One man may be able to do all his will, but the rest will have no will except that which he sees fit to allow them. To put the same point from another side, the first condition of free government is government not by the arbitrary determination of the ruler, but by fixed rules of law, to which the ruler himself is subject. We draw the important inference that there is no essential antithesis between liberty and law. On the contrary, law is essential to liberty. Law, of course, restrains the individual; it is therefore opposed to his liberty at a given moment and in a given direction. But, equally, law restrains others from doing with him as they will. It liberates him from the fear of arbitrary aggression or coercion, and this is the only way, indeed, the only sense, in which liberty *for an entire community* is attainable.

There is one point tacitly postulated in this argument which should not be overlooked. In assuming that the reign of law guarantees liberty to the whole community, we are assuming that it is impartial. If there is one law for the Government and another for its subjects, one for noble and another for commoner, one for rich and another for poor, the law does not guarantee liberty for all. Liberty in this respect implies equality. Hence the demand of Liberalism for such a procedure as will ensure the impartial application of law. Hence the demand for the independence of the judiciary to secure equality as between the Government and its subjects. Hence the demand for cheap procedure and accessible courts. Hence the abolition of privileges of class.[2] Hence will come in time the demand for the abolition of the power of money to purchase skilled advocacy.

2. *Fiscal Liberty.*

Closely connected with juristic liberty, and more widely felt in everyday life, is the question of fiscal liberty. The Stuarts brought things to a head in this country by arbitrary taxation. George III brought things to a head in America by the same infallible method. The immediate cause of the French Revolution was the refusal of the nobles and the clergy to bear their share of the financial burden. But fiscal liberty raises more searching questions than juristic liberty. It is not enough that taxes should be fixed by a law applying universally and impartially, for taxes vary from year to year in accordance with public needs, and while other laws may remain stable and unchanged for an indefinite period, taxation must, in the nature of the case, be adjustable. It is a matter, properly considered, for the Executive rather than the Legislature. Hence the liberty of the subject in fiscal matters means the restraint of the Executive, not merely by established and written laws, but by a more direct and constant supervision. It means, in a word, responsible government, and that is why we have more often heard the cry, "No taxation without representation," than the cry, "No legislation without representation." Hence, from the seventeenth century onwards, fiscal liberty was seen to involve what is called political liberty.

3. *Personal Liberty.*

Of political liberty it will be more convenient to speak later. But let us here observe that there is another avenue by which it can be, and, in fact, was, approached. We have seen that the reign of law is the first step to liberty. A man is not free when he is controlled by other men, but only when he is controlled

---

[2] In England "benefit of clergy" was still a good plea for remission of sentence for a number of crimes in the seventeenth century. At that time all who could read could claim benefit, which was therefore of the nature of a privilege for the educated class. The requirement of reading, which had become a form, was abolished in 1705, but peers and clerks in holy orders could still plead their clergy in the eighteenth century, and the last relics of the privilege were not finally abolished till the nineteenth century.

by principles and rules which all society must obey, for the community is the true master of the free man. But here we are only at the beginning of the matter. There may be law, and there may be no attempt, such as the Stuarts made, to set law aside, yet (1) the making and maintenance of law may depend on the will of the sovereign or of an oligarchy, and (2) the content of the law may be unjust and oppressive to some, to many, or to all except those who make it. The first point brings us back to the problem of political liberty, which we defer. The second opens questions which have occupied a great part of the history of Liberalism, and to deal with them we have to ask what types of law have been felt as peculiarly oppressive, and in what respects it has been necessary to claim liberty not merely through law, but by the abolition of bad law and tyrannical administration.

In the first place, there is the sphere of what is called personal liberty—a sphere most difficult to define, but the arena of the fiercest strife of passion and the deepest feelings of mankind. At the basis lies liberty of thought—freedom from inquisition into opinions that a man forms in his own mind[3]—the inner citadel where, if anywhere, the individual must rule. But liberty of thought is of very little avail without liberty to exchange thoughts—since thought is mainly a social product; and so with liberty of thought goes liberty of speech and liberty of writing, printing, and peaceable discussion. These rights are not free from difficulty and dubiety. There is a point at which speech becomes indistinguishable from action, and free speech may mean the right to create disorder. The limits of just liberty here are easy to draw neither in theory nor in practice. They lead us immediately to one of the points at which liberty and order may be in conflict, and it is with conflicts of this kind that we shall have to deal. The possibilities of conflict are not less in relation to the connected right of liberty in religion. That this liberty is absolute cannot be contended. No modern state would tolerate a form of religious worship which should include cannibalism, human sacrifice, or the burning of witches. In point of fact, practices of this kind—which follow quite naturally from various forms of primitive belief that are most sincerely held—are habitually put down by civilized peoples that are responsible for the government of less developed races. The British law recognizes polygamy in India, but I imagine it would not be open either to a Mahommedan or a Hindu to contract two marriages in England. Nor is it for liberty of this kind that the battle has been fought.

What, then, is the primary meaning of religious liberty? Externally, I take it to include the liberties of thought and expression, and to add to these the right of worship in any form which does not inflict injury on others or involve a breach of public order. This limitation appears to carry with it a certain decency and restraint in expression which avoids unnecessary insult to the feelings of others; and I think this implication must be allowed, though it makes some

---

[3] See an interesting chapter in Faguet's *Liberalisme*, which points out that the common saying that thought is free is negated by any inquisition which compels a man to disclose opinions, and penalizes him if they are not such as to suit the inquisitor.

room for strained and unfair applications. Externally, again, we must note that the demand for religious liberty soon goes beyond mere toleration. Religious liberty is incomplete as long as any belief is penalized, as, for example, by carrying with it exclusion from office or from educational advantages. On this side, again, full liberty implies full equality. Turning to the internal side, the spirit of religious liberty rests on the conception that a man's religion ranks with his own innermost thought and feelings. It is the most concrete expression of his personal attitude to life, to his kind, to the world, to his own origin and destiny. There is no real religion that is not thus drenched in personality; and the more religion is recognized for spiritual the starker the contradiction is felt to be that any one should seek to impose a religion on another. Properly regarded, the attempt is not wicked, but impossible. Yet those sin most against true religion who try to convert men from the outside by mechanical means. They have the lie in the soul, being most ignorant of the nature of that for which they feel most deeply.

Yet here again we stumble on difficulties. Religion is personal. Yet is not religion also eminently social? What is more vital to the social order than its beliefs? If we send a man to gaol for stealing trash, what shall we do to him whom, in our conscience and on our honour, we believe to be corrupting the hearts of mankind, and perhaps leading them to eternal perdition? Again, what in the name of liberty are we to do to men whose preaching, if followed out in act, would bring back the rack and the stake? Once more there is a difficulty of delimitation which will have to be fully sifted. I will only remark here that our practice has arrived at a solution which, upon the whole, appears to have worked well hitherto, and which has its roots in principle. It is open to a man to preach the principles of Torquemada or the religion of Mahomet. It is not open to men to practise such of their precepts as would violate the rights of others or cause a breach of the peace. Expression is free, and worship is free as far as it is the expression of personal devotion. So far as they infringe the freedom, or, more generally, the rights of others, the practices inculcated by a religion cannot enjoy unqualified freedom.

4. *Social Liberty.*

From the spiritual we turn to the practical side of life. On this side we may observe, first, that Liberalism has had to deal with those restraints on the individual which flow from the hierarchic organization of society, and reserve certain offices, certain forms of occupation, and perhaps the right or at least the opportunity of education generally, to people of a certain rank or class. In its more extreme form this is a caste system, and its restrictions are religious or legal as well as social. In Europe it has taken more than one form. There is the monopoly of certain occupations by corporations, prominent in the minds of eighteenth-century French reformers. There is the reservation of public appointments and ecclesiastical patronage for those who are "born," and there is a more subtly pervading spirit of class which produces a hostile attitude to those who could and would rise; and this spirit finds a more material ally in the educational difficulties that beset brains unendowed with wealth. I need not labour points which will be apparent to all, but have again to remark two things. (1) Once more the struggle for liberty is also, when pushed through, a struggle for equality. Freedom to choose and follow an occupation, if it is to become fully effective, means equality with others in the opportunities for following such occupation. This is, in fact, one among the various considerations which lead Liberalism to support a national system of free education, and will lead it further yet on the same lines. (2) Once again, though we may insist on the rights of the individual, the social value of the corporation or quasi-corporation, like the Trade Union, cannot be ignored. Experience shows the necessity of some measure of collective regulation in industrial matters, and in the adjustment of such regulation to individual liberty serious difficulties of principle emerge. We shall have to refer to these in the next section. But one point is relevant at this stage. It is clearly a matter of Liberal principle that membership of a corporation should not depend on any hereditary qualification, nor be set about with any artificial difficulty of entry, where by the term artificial is meant any difficulty not involved in the nature of the occupation concerned, but designed for purposes of exclusiveness. As against all such methods of restriction, the Liberal case is clear.

It has only to be added here that restrictions of sex are in every respect parallel to restrictions of class. There are, doubtless, occupations for which women are unfit. But, if so, the test of fitness is sufficient to exclude them. The "open road for women" is one application, and a very big one, of the "open road for talent," and to secure them both is of the essence of Liberalism.

5. *Economic Liberty*

Apart from monopolies, industry was shackled in the earlier part of the modern period by restrictive legislation in various forms, by navigation laws, and by tariffs. In particular, the tariff was not merely an obstruction to free enterprise, but a source of inequality as between trade and trade. Its fundamental effect is to transfer capital and labour from the objects on which they can be most profitably employed in a given locality, to objects on which they are less profitably employed, by endowing certain industries to the disadvantage of the general consumer. Here, again, the Liberal movement is at once an attack on an obstruction and on an inequality. In most countries the attack has succeeded in breaking down local tariffs and establishing relatively large Free Trade units. It is only in England, and only owing to our early manufacturing supremacy, that it has fully succeeded in overcoming the Protective principle, and even in England the Protectionist reaction would undoubtedly have gained at least a temporary victory but for our dependence on foreign countries for food and the materials of industry. The most striking victory of Liberal ideas is one of the most precarious. At the same time, the battle is one which Liberalism is always prepared to fight over again. It has led to no back stroke, no counter-movement within the Liberal ranks themselves.

It is otherwise with organized restrictions upon industry. The old regulations, which were quite unsuited to the conditions of the time, either fell into desuetude during the eighteenth century, or were formally abolished during the earlier years of the industrial revolution. For a while it seemed as though wholly unrestricted industrial enterprise was to be the progressive watchword, and the echoes of that time still linger. But the old restrictions had not been formally withdrawn before a new process of regulation began. The conditions produced by the new factory system shocked the public conscience; and as early as 1802 we find the first of a long series of laws, out of which has grown an industrial code that year by year follows the life of the operative, in his relations with his employer, into more minute detail. The first stages of this movement were contemplated with doubt and distrust by many men of Liberal sympathies. The intention was, doubtless, to protect the weaker party, but the method was that of interference with freedom of contract. Now the freedom of the sane adult individual—even such strong individualists as Cobden recognized that the case of children stood apart—carried with it the right of concluding such agreements as seemed best to suit his own interests, and involved both the right and the duty of determining the lines of his life for himself. Free contract and personal responsibility lay close to the heart of the whole Liberal movement. Hence the doubts felt by so many Liberals as to the regulation of industry by law. None the less, as time has gone on, men of the keenest Liberal sympathies have come not merely to accept but eagerly to advance the extension of public control in the industrial sphere, and of collective responsibility in the matter of the education and even the feeding of children, the housing of the industrial population, the care of the sick and aged, the provision of the means of regular employment. On this side Liberalism seems definitely to have retraced its steps, and we shall have to inquire closely into the question whether the reversal is a change of principle or of application.

Closely connected with freedom of contract is freedom of association. If men may make any agreement with one another in their mutual interest so long as they do not injure a third party, they may apparently agree to act together permanently for any purposes of common interest on the same conditions. That is, they may form associations. Yet at bottom the powers of an association are something very different from the powers of the individuals composing it; and it is only by legal pedantry that the attempt can be made to regulate the behaviour of an association on principles derived from and suitable to the relations of individuals. An association might become so powerful as to form a state within the state, and to contend with government on no unequal terms. The history of some revolutionary societies, of some ecclesiastical organizations, even of some American trusts might be quoted to show that the danger is not imaginary. Short of this, an association may act oppressively towards others and even towards its own members, and the function of Liberalism may be rather to protect the individual against the power of the association than to protect the right of association against the restriction of the law. In fact, in this regard, the principle of liberty cuts both ways, and this double application is reflected in history. The emancipation of trade unions, however, extending over the period from 1824 to 1906, and perhaps not yet complete, was in the main a liberating movement, because combination was necessary to place the workman on something approaching terms of equality with the employer, and because tacit combinations of employers could never, in fact, be prevented by law. It was, again, a movement to liberty through equality. On the other hand, the oppressive capacities of a trade union could never be left out of account, while combinations of capital, which might be infinitely more powerful, have justly been regarded with distrust. In this there is no inconsistency of principle, but a just appreciation of a real difference of circumstance. Upon the whole it may be said that the function of Liberalism is not so much to maintain a general right of free association as to define the right in each case in such terms as make for the maximum of real liberty and equality.

6. *Domestic Liberty.*

Of all associations within the State, the miniature community of the Family is the most universal and of the strongest independent vitality. The authoritarian state was reflected in the authoritarian family, in which the husband was within wide limits absolute lord of the person and property of wife and children. The movement of liberation consists (1) in rendering the wife a fully responsible individual, capable of holding property, suing and being sued, conducting business on her own account, and enjoying full personal protection against her husband; (2) in establishing marriage as far as the law is concerned on a purely contractual basis, and leaving the sacramental aspect of marriage to the ordinances of the religion professed by the parties; (3) in securing the physical, mental, and moral care of the children, partly by imposing definite responsibilities on the parents and punishing them for neglect, partly by elaborating a public system of education and of hygiene. The first two movements are sufficiently typical cases of the interdependence of liberty and equality. The third is more often conceived as a Socialistic than a Liberal tendency, and, in point of fact, the State control of education gives rise to some searching questions of principle, which have not yet been fully solved. If, in general, education is a duty which the State has a right to enforce, there is a countervailing right of choice as to the lines of education which it would be ill to ignore, and the mode of adjustment has not yet been adequately determined either in theory or in practice. I would, however, strongly maintain that the general conception of the State as Over-parent is quite as truly Liberal as Socialistic. It is the basis of the rights of the child, of his protection against parental neglect, of the equality of opportunity which he may claim as a future citizen, of his training to fill his place as a grown-up person in the social system. Liberty once more involves control and restraint.

7. *Local, Racial, and National Liberty.*

From the smallest social unit we pass to the largest. A great part of the liberating movement is occupied with the struggle of entire nations against alien rule, with the revolt of Europe against Napoleon, with the struggle of Italy for freedom, with the fate of the Christian subjects of Turkey, with the emancipation of the negro, with the national movement in Ireland and in India. Many of these struggles present the problem of liberty in its simplest form. It has been and is too often a question of securing the most elementary rights for the weaker party; and those who are not touched by the appeal are deficient rather in imagination than in logic or ethics. But at the back of national movements very difficult questions do arise. What is a nation as distinct from a state? What sort of unity does it constitute, and what are its rights? If Ireland is a nation, is Ulster one? and if Ulster is a British and Protestant nation, what of the Catholic half of Ulster? History has in some cases given us a practical answer. Thus, it has shown that, enjoying the gift of responsible government, French and British, despite all historical quarrels and all differences of religious belief, language, and social structure, have fused into the nation of Canada. History has justified the conviction that Germany was a nation, and thrown ridicule on the contemptuous saying of Metternich that Italy was a geographical expression. But how to anticipate history, what rights to concede to a people that claims to be a self-determining unit, is less easy to decide. There is no doubt that the general tendency of Liberalism is to favour autonomy, but, faced as it is with the problems of subdivision and the complexity of group with group, it has to rely on the concrete teaching of history and the practical insight of statesmanship to determine how the lines of autonomy are to be drawn. There is, however, one empirical test which seems generally applicable. Where a weaker nation incorporated with a larger or stronger one can be governed by ordinary law applicable to both parties to the union, and fulfilling all the ordinary principles of liberty, the arrangement may be the best for both parties. But where this system fails, where the government is constantly forced to resort to exceptional legislation or perhaps to de-liberalize its own institutions, the case becomes urgent. Under such conditions the most liberally-minded democracy is maintaining a system which must undermine its own principles. The Assyrian conqueror, Mr. Herbert Spencer remarks, who is depicted in the bas-reliefs leading his captive by a cord, is bound with that cord himself. He forfeits his liberty as long as he retains his power.

Somewhat similar questions arise about race, which many people wrongly confuse with nationality. So far as elementary rights are concerned there can be no question as to the attitude of Liberalism. When the political power which should guarantee such rights is brought into view, questions of fact arise. Is the Negro or the Kaffir mentally and morally capable of self-government or of taking part in a self-governing State? The experience of Cape Colony tends to the affirmative view. American experience of the negro gives, I take it, a more doubtful answer. A specious extension of the white man's rights to the black may be the best way of ruining the black. To destroy tribal custom by introducing conceptions of individual property, the free disposal of land, and the free purchase of gin may be the handiest method for the expropriator. In all relations with weaker peoples we move in an atmosphere vitiated by the insincere use of high-sounding words. If men say equality, they mean oppression by forms of justice. If they say tutelage, they appear to mean the kind of tutelage extended to the fattened goose. In such an atmosphere, perhaps, our safest course, so far as principles and deductions avail at all, is to fix our eyes on the elements of the matter, and in any part of the world to support whatever method succeeds in securing the "coloured" man from personal violence, from the lash, from expropriation, and from gin; above all, so far as it may yet be, from the white man himself. Until the white man has fully learnt to rule his own life, the best of all things that he can do with the dark man is to do nothing with him. In this relation, the day of a more constructive Liberalism is yet to come.

8. *International Liberty.*

If non-interference is the best thing for the barbarian many Liberals have thought it to be the supreme wisdom in international affairs generally. I shall examine this view later. Here I merely remark: (1) It is of the essence of Liberalism to oppose the use of force, the basis of all tyranny. (2) It is one of its practical necessities to withstand the tyranny of armaments. Not only may the military force be directly turned against liberty, as in Russia, but there are more subtle ways, as in Western Europe, in which the military spirit eats into free institutions and absorbs the public resources which might go to the advancement of civilization. (3) In proportion as the world becomes free, the use of force becomes meaningless. There is no purpose in aggression if it is not to issue in one form or another of national subjection.

9. *Political Liberty and Popular Sovereignty.*

Underlying all these questions of right is the question how they are to be secured and maintained. By enforcing the responsibility of the executive and legislature to the community as a whole? Such is the general answer, and it indicates one of the lines of connection between the general theory of liberty and the doctrine of universal suffrage and the sovereignty of the people. The answer, however, does not meet all the possibilities of the case. The people as a whole might be careless of their rights and incapable of managing them. They might be set on the conquest of others, the expropriation of the rich, or on any form of collective tyranny or folly. It is perfectly possible that from the point of view of general liberty and social progress a limited franchise might give better results than one that is more extended. Even in this country it is a tenable view that the extension of the suffrage in 1884 tended for some years to arrest the development of liberty in various directions. On what theory does the principle of popular sovereignty rest, and within what limits does it hold good? Is it a part of the general principles of liberty and equality, or are other ideas involved? These are among the questions which we shall have to examine.

We have now passed the main phases of the Liberal movement in very summary review, and we have noted, first, that it is co-extensive with life. It is concerned with the individual, the family, the State. It touches industry, law, religion, ethics. It would not be difficult, if space allowed, to illustrate its influence in literature and art, to describe the war with convention, insincerity, and patronage, and the struggle for free self-expression, for reality, for the artist's soul. Liberalism is an all-penetrating element of the life-structure of the modern world. Secondly, it is an effective historical force. If its work is nowhere complete, it is almost everywhere in progress. The modern State as we see it in Europe outside Russia, in the British colonies, in North and South America, as we begin to see it in the Russian empire and throughout the vast continent of

Asia, is the old authoritarian society modified in greater or less degree by the absorption of Liberal principles. Turning, thirdly, to those principles themselves, we have recognized Liberalism in every department as a movement fairly denoted by the name—a movement of liberation, a clearance of obstructions, an opening of channels for the flow of free spontaneous vital activity. Fourthly, we have seen that in a large number of cases what is under one aspect a movement for liberty is on another side a movement towards equality, and the habitual association of these principles is so far confirmed. On the other hand, lastly, we have seen numerous cases in which the exacter definition of liberty and the precise meaning of equality remain obscure, and to discuss these will be our task. We have, moreover, admittedly regarded Liberalism mainly in its earlier and more negative aspect. We have seen it as a force working within an old society and modifying it by the loosening of the bonds which its structure imposed on human activity. We have yet to ask what constructive social scheme, if any, could be formed on Liberal principles; and it is here, if at all, that the fuller meaning of the principles of Liberty and Equality should appear, and the methods of applying them be made out. The problem of popular sovereignty pointed to the same need. Thus the lines of the remainder of our task are clearly laid down. We have to get at the fundamentals of Liberalism, and to consider what kind of structure can be raised upon the basis which they offer. We will approach the question by tracing the historic movement of Liberal thought through certain well-marked phases. We shall see how the problems which have been indicated were attacked by successive thinkers, and how partial solutions gave occasion for deeper probings. Following the guidance of the actual movement of ideas, we shall reach the centre and heart of Liberalism, and we shall try to form a conception of the essentials of the Liberal creed as a constructive theory of society. This conception we shall then apply to the greater questions, political and economic, of our own day; and this will enable us finally to estimate the present position of Liberalism as a living force in the modern world and the prospect of transforming its ideals into actualities.

CHAPTER III

THE MOVEMENT OF THEORY

Great changes are not caused by ideas alone; but they are not effected without ideas. The passions of men must be aroused if the frost of custom is to be broken or the chains of authority burst; but passion of itself is blind and its world is chaotic. To be effective men must act together, and to act together they must have a common understanding and a common object. When it comes to be a question of any far-reaching change, they must not merely conceive their own immediate end with clearness. They must convert others, they must communicate sympathy and win over the unconvinced. Upon the whole, they must show that their object is possible, that it is compatible with existing institutions, or at any rate with some workable form of social life. They are, in fact, driven on by the requirements of their position to the elaboration of ideas, and in the end to some sort of social philosophy; and the philosophies that have driving force behind them are those which arise after this fashion out of the practical demands of human feeling. The philosophies that remain ineffectual and academic are those that are formed by abstract reflection without relation to the thirsty souls of human kind.

In England, it is true, where men are apt to be shy and unhandy in the region of theory, the Liberal movement has often sought to dispense with general principles. In its early days and in its more moderate forms, it sought its ends under the guise of constitutionalism. As against the claims of the Stuart monarchy, there was a historic case as well as a philosophic argument, and the earlier leaders of the Parliament relied more on precedent than on principle. This method was embodied in the Whig tradition, and runs on to our own time, as one of the elements that go to make up the working constitution of the Liberal mind. It is, so to say, the Conservative element in Liberalism, valuable in resistance to encroachments, valuable in securing continuity of development, for purposes of re-construction insufficient. To maintain the old order under changed circumstances may be, in fact, to initiate a revolution. It was so in the seventeenth century. Pym and his followers could find justification for their contentions in our constitutional history, but to do so they had to go behind both the Stuarts and the Tudors; and to apply the principles of the fourteenth and fifteenth centuries in 1640 was, in effect, to institute a revolution. In our own time, to maintain the right of the Commons against the Lords is, on the face of it, to adhere to old constitutional right, but to do so under the new circumstances which have made the Commons representative of the nation as a whole is, in reality, to establish democracy for the first time on a firm footing, and this, again, is to accomplish a revolution.

Now, those who effect a revolution ought to know whither they are leading the world. They have need of a social theory—and in point of fact the more thorough-going apostles of movement always have such a theory; and though, as we have remarked, the theory emerges from the practical needs which they feel, and is therefore apt to invest ideas of merely temporary value with the character of eternal truths, it is not on this account to be dismissed as of secondary importance. Once formed, it reacts upon the minds of its adherents, and gives direction and unity to their efforts. It becomes, in its turn, a real historic force, and the degree of its coherence and adequacy is matter, not merely of academic interest, but of practical moment. Moreover, the onward course of a movement is more clearly understood by appreciating the successive points of view which its thinkers and statesmen have occupied than by following the devious turnings of political events and the tangle of party controversy. The point of view naturally affects the whole method of handling problems, whether speculative or practical, and to the historian it serves as a centre around which ideas and policies that perhaps differ, and even conflict with one another, may be so grouped as to show their underlying affinities. Let us then seek to determine the principal points of view which the Liberal movement has occupied, and distinguish the main types of theory in which the passion for freedom has sought to express itself.

The first of these types I will call the theory of the Natural Order.

The earlier Liberalism had to deal with authoritarian government in church and state. It had to vindicate the elements of personal, civil, and economic freedom; and in so doing it took its stand on the rights of man, and, in proportion as it was forced to be constructive, on the supposed harmony of the natural order. Government claimed supernatural sanction and divine ordinance. Liberal theory replied in effect that the rights of man rested on the law of Nature, and those of government on human institution. The oldest "institution" in this view was the individual, and the primordial society the natural grouping of human beings under the influence of family affection, and for the sake of mutual aid. Political society was a more artificial arrangement, a convention arrived at for the specific purpose of securing a better order and maintaining the common safety. It was, perhaps, as Locke held, founded on a contract between king and people, a contract which was brought to an end if either party violated its terms. Or, as in Rousseau's view, it was essentially a contract of the people with one another, an arrangement by means of which, out of many conflicting individual wills, a common or general will could be formed. A government might be instituted as the organ of this will, but it would, from the nature of the case, be subordinate to the people from whom it derived authority. The people were sovereign. The government was their delegate.

Whatever the differences of outlook that divide these theories, those who from Locke to Rousseau and Paine worked with this order of ideas agreed in conceiving political society as a restraint to which men voluntarily submitted themselves for specific purposes. Political institutions were the source of subjection and inequality. Before and behind them stood the assemblage of free and equal individuals. But the isolated individual was powerless. He had rights which were limited only by the corresponding rights of others, but he could not, unless chance gave him the upper hand, enforce them. Accordingly, he found it best to enter into an arrangement with others for the mutual respect of rights;

and for this purpose he instituted a government to maintain his rights within the community and to guard the community from assault from without. It followed that the function of government was limited and definable. It was to maintain the natural rights of man as accurately as the conditions of society allowed, and to do naught beside. Any further action employing the compulsory power of the State was of the nature of an infringement of the understanding on which government rested. In entering into the compact, the individual gave up so much of his rights as was necessitated by the condition of submitting to a common rule—so much, and no more. He gave up his natural rights and received in return civil rights, something less complete, perhaps, but more effective as resting on the guarantee of the collective power. If you would discover, then, what the civil rights of man in society should be, you must inquire what are the natural rights of man,[4] and how far they are unavoidably modified in accommodating the conflicting claims of men with one another. Any interference that goes beyond this necessary accommodation is oppression. Civil rights should agree as nearly as possible with natural rights, or, as Paine says, a civil right is a natural right exchanged.

This conception of the relations of the State and the individual long outlived the theory on which it rested. It underlies the entire teaching of the Manchester school. Its spirit was absorbed, as we shall see, by many of the Utilitarians. It operated, though in diminishing force, throughout the nineteenth century; and it is strongly held by contemporary Liberals like M. Faguet, who frankly abrogate its speculative foundations and rest their case on social utility. Its strength is, in effect, not in its logical principles, but in the compactness and consistency which it gives to a view of the functions of the State which responds to certain needs of modern society. As long as those needs were uppermost, the theory was of living value. In proportion as they have been satisfied and other needs have emerged, the requirement has arisen for a fuller and sounder principle.

But there was another side to the theory of nature which we must not ignore. If in this theory government is the marplot and authority the source of oppression and stagnation, where are the springs of progress and civilization? Clearly, in the action of individuals. The more the individual receives free scope for the play of his faculties, the more rapidly will society as a whole advance. There are here the elements of an important truth, but what is the implication? If the individual is free, any two individuals, each pursuing his own ends, may find themselves in conflict. It was, in fact, the possibility of such conflict which was recognized by our theory as the origin and foundation of society. Men had to agree to some measure of mutual restraint in order that their liberty might be effective. But in the course of the eighteenth century, and particularly in the

---

[4] *Cf.* the preamble to the Declaration of the Rights of Man by the French National Assembly in 1789. The Assembly lays down "the natural, inalienable, and sacred rights of man," in order, among other things, "that the acts of the legislative power and those of the executive power, being capable of being at every instant compared with the end of every political institution, may be more respected accordingly."

economic sphere, there arose a view that the conflict of wills is based on misunderstanding and ignorance, and that its mischiefs are accentuated by governmental repression. At bottom there is a natural harmony of interests. Maintain external order, suppress violence, assure men in the possession of their property, and enforce the fulfilment of contracts, and the rest will go of itself. Each man will be guided by self-interest, but interest will lead him along the lines of greatest productivity. If all artificial barriers are removed, he will find the occupation which best suits his capacities, and this will be the occupation in which he will be most productive, and therefore, socially, most valuable. He will have to sell his goods to a willing purchaser, therefore he must devote himself to the production of things which others need, things, therefore, of social value. He will, by preference, make that for which he can obtain the highest price, and this will be that for which, at the particular time and place and in relation to his particular capacities, there is the greatest need. He will, again, find the employer who will pay him best, and that will be the employer to whom he can do the best service. Self-interest, if enlightened and unfettered, will, in short, lead him to conduct coincident with public interest. There is, in this sense, a natural harmony between the individual and society. True, this harmony might require a certain amount of education and enlightenment to make it effective. What it did not require was governmental "interference," which would always hamper the causes making for its smooth and effectual operation. Government must keep the ring, and leave it for individuals to play out the game. The theory of the natural rights of the individual is thus supplemented by a theory of the mutual harmony of individual and social needs, and, so completed, forms a conception of human society which is *primâ facie* workable, which, in fact, contains important elements of truth, and which was responsive to the needs of a great class, and to many of the requirements of society as a whole, during a considerable period.

On both sides, however, the theory exhibits, under criticism, fundamental weaknesses which have both a historical and a speculative significance. Let us first consider the conception of natural rights. What were these rights, and on what did they rest? On the first point men sought to be explicit. By way of illustration we cannot do better than quote the leading clauses of the Declaration of 1789.[5]

Article I.—Men are born and remain free and equal in rights. Social distinctions can only be founded on common utility.

Article II.—The end of every political association is the conservation of the natural and imprescriptible rights of man.[6] These rights are liberty, property, security (*la sûreté*), and resistance to oppression.

---

[5] The comparison of the Declaration of the Assembly in 1789 with that of the Convention in 1793 is full of interest, both for the points of agreement and difference, but would require a lengthy examination. I note one or two points in passing.

[6] Contrast 1793, Art. I: "The end of society is the common happiness. Government is instituted to guarantee to man the enjoyment of his natural and imprescriptible rights."

Article III.—The principle of all sovereignty resides essentially in the nation....

Article IV.—Liberty consists in the power to do anything that does not injure others; thus, the exercise of the natural rights of every man has only such limits as assure to other members of society the enjoyment of the same rights. These limits can only be determined by law.

Article VI.—The law is the expression of the general will. All citizens have a right to take part (*concourir*), personally or by their representatives, in its formation.

The remainder of this article insists on the impartiality of law and the equal admission of all citizens to office. The Declaration of 1793 is more emphatic about equality, and more rhetorical. Article III reads, "All men are equal by nature and before the law."

It is easy to subject these articles to a niggling form of criticism in which their spirit is altogether missed. I would ask attention only to one or two points of principle.

(*a*) What are the rights actually claimed? "Security" and "resistance to oppression" are not in principle distinct, and, moreover, may be taken as covered by the definition of liberty. The meaning at bottom is "Security for liberty in respect of his person and property is the right of every man." So expressed, it will be seen that this right postulates the existence of an ordered society, and lays down that it is the duty of such a society to secure the liberty of its members. The right of the individual, then, is not something independent of society, but one of the principles which a good social order must recognize.

(*b*) Observe that equality is limited by the "common utility," and that the sphere of liberty is ultimately to be defined by "law." In both cases we are referred back from the individual either to the needs or to the decision of society as a whole. There are, moreover, two definitions of liberty. (1) It is the power to do what does not injure others. (2) It is a right limited by the consideration that others must enjoy the same rights. It is important to bear in mind that these two definitions are highly discrepant. If my right to knock a man down is only limited by his equal right to knock me down, the law has no business to interfere when we take to our fists. If, on the other hand, I have no right to injure another, the law should interfere. Very little reflection suffices to show that this is the sounder principle, and that respect for the equal liberty of another is not an adequate definition of liberty. My right to keep my neighbour awake by playing the piano all night is not satisfactorily counterbalanced by his right to keep a dog which howls all the time the piano is being played. The right of a "sweater" to pay starvation wages is not satisfactorily limited by the corresponding right which his employee would enjoy if he were in a position to impose the same terms on some one else. Generally, the right to injure or take advantage of another is not sufficiently limited by the right of that other if he should have the power to retaliate in kind. There is no right to injure another; and if we ask what is injury we are again thrown back on some general principle which will override the individual claim to do what one will.

(c) The doctrine of popular sovereignty rests on two principles. (1) It is said to reside in the nation. Law is the expression of the general will. Here the "nation" is conceived as a collective whole, as a unit. (2) Every citizen has the right to take part in making the law. Here the question is one of individual right. Which is the real ground of democratic representation—the unity of the national life, or the inherent right of the individual to be consulted about that which concerns himself?

Further, and this is a very serious question, which is the ultimate authority—the will of the nation, or the rights of the individual? Suppose the nation deliberately decides on laws which deny the rights of the individual, ought such laws to be obeyed in the name of popular sovereignty, or to be disobeyed in the name of natural rights? It is a real issue, and on these lines it is unfortunately quite insoluble.

These difficulties were among the considerations which led to the formation of the second type of Liberal theory, and what has to be said about the harmony of the natural order may be taken in conjunction with this second theory to which we may now pass, and which is famous as The Greatest Happiness Principle.

Bentham, who spent the greater part of his life in elaborating the greatest happiness principle as a basis of social reconstruction, was fully alive to the difficulties which we have found in the theory of natural rights. The alleged rights of man were for him so many anarchical fallacies. They were founded on no clearly assignable principle, and admitted of no demonstration. "I say I have a right." "I say you have no such right." Between the disputants who or what is to decide? What was the supposed law of nature? When was it written, and by whose authority? On what ground do we maintain that men are free or equal? On what principle and within what limits do we or can we maintain the right of property? There were points on which, by universal admission, all these rights have to give way. What is the right of property worth in times of war or of any overwhelming general need? The Declaration itself recognized the need of appeal to common utility or to the law to define the limits of individual right. Bentham would frankly make all rights dependent on common utility, and therewith he would make it possible to examine all conflicting claims in the light of a general principle. He would measure them all by a common standard. Has a man the right to express his opinion freely? To determine the question on Bentham's lines we must ask whether it is, on the whole, useful to society that the free expression of opinion should be allowed, and this, he would say, is a question which may be decided by general reasoning and by experience of results. Of course, we must take the rough with the smooth. If the free expression of opinion is allowed, false opinion will find utterance and will mislead many. The question would be, does the loss involved in the promulgation of error counterbalance the gain to be derived from unfettered discussion? and Bentham would hold himself free to judge by results. Should the State maintain the rights of private property? Yes, if the admission of those rights is useful to the community as a whole. No, if it is not useful. Some rights of property, again, may be advantageous, others disadvantageous. The community is free to make a selection. If it finds that certain forms of property are working to the exclusive benefit of individuals and the prejudice of the common weal, it has good ground for the suppression of those forms of property, while it may, with equal justice, maintain other forms of property which it holds sound as judged by the effect on the common welfare. It is limited by no "imprescriptible" right of the individual. It may do with the individual what it pleases provided that it has the good of the whole in view. So far as the question of right is concerned the Benthamite principle might be regarded as decidedly socialistic or even authoritarian. It contemplates, at least as a possibility, the complete subordination of individual to social claims.

There is, however, another side to the Benthamite principle, to understand which we must state the heads of the theory itself as a positive doctrine. What is this social utility of which we have spoken? In what does it consist? What is useful to society, and what harmful? The answer has the merit of great clearness and simplicity. An action is good which tends to promote the greatest possible happiness of the greatest possible number of those affected by it. As with an action, so, of course, with an institution or a social system. That is useful which conforms to this principle. That is harmful which conflicts with it. That is right which conforms to it, that is wrong which conflicts with it. The greatest happiness principle is the one and supreme principle of conduct. Observe that it imposes on us two considerations. One is the *greatest* happiness. Now happiness is defined as consisting positively in the presence of pleasure, negatively in the absence of pain. A greater pleasure is then preferable to a lesser, a pleasure unaccompanied by pain to one involving pain. Conceiving pain as a minus quantity of pleasure, we may say that the principle requires us always to take quantity and pleasure into account, and nothing else. But, secondly, the *number* of individuals affected is material. An act might cause pleasure to one and pain to two. Then it is wrong, unless, indeed, the pleasure were very great and the pain in each case small. We must balance the consequences, taking all individuals affected into account, and "everybody must count for one and nobody for more than one." This comment is an integral part of the original formula. As between the happiness of his father, his child, or himself, and the happiness of a stranger, a man must be impartial. He must only consider the quantity of pleasure secured or pain inflicted.

Now, in this conception of measurable quantities of pleasure and pain there is, as many critics have insisted, something unreal and academic. We shall have to return to the point, but let us first endeavour to understand the bearing of Bentham's teaching on the problems of his own time and on the subsequent development of Liberal thought. For this purpose we will keep to what is real in his doctrine, even if it is not always defined with academic precision. The salient points that we note, then, are (1) the subordination of all considerations of right to the considerations of happiness, (2) the importance of number, and (3) as the other side of the same doctrine, the insistence on equality or impartiality between man and man. The common utility which Bentham considers is the happiness experienced by a number of individuals, all of whom are reckoned for this purpose as of equal value. This is the radical individualism of the Benthamite creed, to be set against that socialistic tendency which struck us in our preliminary account.

In this individualism, equality is fundamental. Everybody is to count for one, nobody for more than one, for every one can feel pain and pleasure. Liberty, on the other hand, is not fundamental, it is a means to an end. Popular sovereignty is not fundamental, for all government is a means to an end. Nevertheless, the school of Bentham, upon the whole, stood by both liberty and democracy. Let us consider their attitude.

As to popular government, Bentham and James Mill reasoned after this fashion. Men, if left to themselves, that is to say, if neither trained by an educational discipline nor checked by responsibility, do not consider the good of the greatest number. They consider their own good. A king, if his power is unchecked, will rule in his own interest. A class, if its power is unchecked, will rule in its own interest. The only way to secure fair consideration for the happiness of all is to allow to all an equal share of power. True, if there is a conflict the majority will prevail, but they will be moved each by consideration of his own happiness, and the majority as a whole, therefore, by the happiness of the greater number. There is no inherent right in the individual to take a part in government. There is a claim to be considered in the distribution of the means of happiness, and to share in the work of government as a means to this end. It would follow, among other things, that if one man or one class could be shown to be so much wiser and better than others that his or their rule would, in fact, conduce more to the happiness of the greater number than a popular system, then the business of government ought to be entrusted to that man or that class and no one else ought to interfere with it.

The whole argument, however, implies a crude view of the problem of government. It is, of course, theoretically possible that a question should present itself, detached from other questions, in which a definite measurable interest of each of the seven millions or more of voters is at stake. For example, the great majority of English people drink tea. Comparatively few drink wine. Should a particular sum be raised by a duty on tea or on wine? Here the majority of tea-drinkers have a measurable interest, the same in kind and roughly the same in degree for each; and the vote of the majority, if it could be taken on this question alone and based on self-interest alone, might be conceived without absurdity as representing a sum of individual interests. Even here, however, observe that, though the greatest number is considered, the greatest happiness does not fare so well. For to raise the same sum the tax on wine will, as less is drunk, have to be much larger than the tax on tea, so that a little gain to many tea-drinkers might inflict a heavy loss on the few wine-drinkers, and on the Benthamite principle it is not clear that this would be just. In point of fact it is possible for a majority to act tyrannically, by insisting on a slight convenience to itself at the expense, perhaps, of real suffering to a minority. Now the Utilitarian principle by no means justifies such tyranny, but it does seem to contemplate the weighing of one man's loss against another's gain, and such a method of balancing does not at bottom commend itself to our sense of justice. We may lay down that if there is a rational social order at all it must be one which never rests the essential indispensable condition of the happiness of one man on the unavoidable misery of another, nor the happiness of forty millions of men on the misery of one. It may be temporarily expedient, but it is eternally unjust, that one man should die for the people.

We may go further. The case of the contemplated tax is, as applied to the politics of a modern State, an unreal one. Political questions cannot be thus isolated. Even if we could vote by referendum on a special tax, the question which voters would have to consider would never be the revenue from and the incidence of that tax alone. All the indirect social and economic bearings of the tax would come up for consideration, and in the illustration chosen people would be swayed, and rightly swayed, by their opinion, for example, of the comparative effects of tea-drinking and wine-drinking. No one element of the social life stands separate from the rest, any more than any one element of the animal body stands separate from the rest. In this sense the life of society is rightly held to be organic, and all considered public policy must be conceived in its bearing on the life of society as a whole. But the moment that we apply this view to politics, the Benthamite mode of stating the case for democracy is seen to be insufficient. The interests of every man are no doubt in the end bound up with the welfare of the whole community, but the relation is infinitely subtle and indirect. Moreover, it takes time to work itself out, and the evil that is done in the present day may only bear fruit when the generation that has done it has passed away. Thus, the direct and calculable benefit of the majority may by no means coincide with the ultimate good of society as a whole; and to suppose that the majority must, on grounds of self-interest, govern in the interests of the community as a whole is in reality to attribute to the mass of men full insight into problems which tax the highest efforts of science and of statesmanship. Lastly, to suppose that men are governed entirely by a sense of their interests is a many-sided fallacy. Men are neither so intelligent nor so selfish. They are swayed by emotion and by impulse, and both for good and for evil they will lend enthusiastic support to courses of public policy from which, as individuals, they have nothing to gain. To understand the real value of democratic government, we shall have to probe far deeper into the relations of the individual and society.

I turn lastly to the question of liberty. On Benthamite principles there could be no question here of indefeasible individual right. There were even, as we saw, possibilities of a thorough-going Socialism or of an authoritarian paternalism in the Benthamite principle. But two great considerations told in the opposite direction. One arose from the circumstances of the day. Bentham, originally a man of somewhat conservative temper, was driven into Radicalism comparatively late in life by the indifference or hostility of the governing classes to his schemes of reform. Government, as he saw it, was of the nature of a close corporation with a vested interest hostile to the public weal, and his work is penetrated by distrust of power as such. There was much in the history of the time to justify his attitude. It was difficult at that time to believe in an honest officialdom putting the commonwealth above every personal or corporate interest, and reformers naturally looked to individual initiative as the source of progress. Secondly, and this was a more philosophic argument, the individual was supposed to understand his own interest best, and as the common good was the sum of individual interests, it followed that so far as every man was free to seek his own good, the good of the greatest number would be most effectually realized by general freedom of choice. That there were difficulties in reconciling self-interest with the general good was not denied. But men like James Mill, who especially worked at this side of the problem, held that they could be overcome by moral education. Trained from childhood to associate the good of others with his own, a man would come, he thought, to care for the happiness of others as for the happiness of self. For, in the long run, the two things were coincident. Particularly in a free economic system, as remarked above, each individual, moving along the line of greatest personal profit, would be found to fulfil the function of greatest profit to society. Let this be understood, and we should have true social harmony based on the spontaneous operation of personal interest enlightened by intelligence and chastened by the discipline of unruly instinct.

Thus, though their starting-point was different, the Benthamites arrived at practical results not notably divergent from those of the doctrine of natural liberty; and, on the whole, the two influences worked together in the formation of that school who in the reform period exercised so notable an influence on English Liberalism, and to whose work we must now turn.

CHAPTER IV

'LAISSEZ-FAIRE'

The school of Cobden is affiliated in general outlook both to the doctrine of natural liberty and to the discipline of Bentham. It shared with the Benthamites the thoroughly practical attitude dear to the English mind. It has much less to say of natural rights than the French theorists. On the other hand, it is saturated with the conviction that the unfettered action of the individual is the mainspring of all progress.[7] Its starting-point is economic. Trade is still in fetters. The worst of the archaic internal restrictions have, indeed, been thrown off. But even here Cobden is active in the work of finally emancipating Manchester from manorial rights that have no place in the nineteenth century. The main work, however, is the liberation of foreign trade. The Corn Laws, as even the tariff reformers of our own day admit, were conceived in the interest of the governing classes. They frankly imposed a tax on the food of the masses for the benefit of the landlords, and as the result of the agricultural and industrial revolutions which had been in progress since 1760, the masses had been brought to the lowest point of economic misery. Give to every man the right to buy in the cheapest and sell in the dearest market, urged the Cobdenite, and trade would automatically expand. The business career would be open to the talents. The good workman would command the full money's worth of his work, and his money would buy him food and clothing at the lowest rate in the world's market. Only so would he get the full value of his work, paying toll to none. Taxes there must be to carry on government, but if we looked into the cost of government we found that it depended mostly on armaments. Why did we need armaments? First, because of the national antagonisms aroused and maintained by a protective system. Free commercial intercourse between nations would engender mutual knowledge, and knit the severed peoples by countless ties of business interests. Free Trade meant peace, and once taught by the example of Great Britain's prosperity, other nations would follow suit, and Free Trade would be universal. The other root of national danger was the principle of intervention. We took it on ourselves to set other nations right. How could we judge for other nations? Force was no remedy. Let every people be free to work out its own salvation. Things were not so perfect with us that we need go about setting the houses of other people in order. To complete personal freedom, there must be national freedom. There must also be colonial freedom. The colonies could no longer be governed in the interests of the mother country, nor ought they to require standing garrisons

---

[7] "If I were asked to sum up in a sentence the difference and the connection (between the two schools) I would say that the Manchester men were the disciples of Adam Smith and Bentham, while the Philosophical Radicals followed Bentham and Adam Smith" (F. W. Hirst, *The Manchester School*, Introd., p. xi). Lord Morley, in the concluding chapter of his *Life of Cobden*, points out that it was the view of "policy as a whole" in connection with the economic movement of society which distinguished the school of Cobden from that of the Benthamites.

maintained by the mother country. They were distant lands, each, if we gave it freedom, with a great future of its own, capable of protecting itself, and developing with freedom into true nationhood. Personal freedom, colonial freedom, international freedom, were parts of one whole. Non-intervention, peace, restriction of armaments, retrenchment of expenditure, reduction of taxation, were the connected series of practical consequences. The money retrenched from wasteful military expenditure need not all be remitted to the taxpayer. A fraction of it devoted to education—free, secular, and universal—would do as much good as when spent on guns and ships it did harm. For education was necessary to raise the standard of intelligence, and provide the substantial equality of opportunity at the start without which the mass of men could not make use of the freedom given by the removal of legislative restrictions. There were here elements of a more constructive view for which Cobden and his friends have not always received sufficient credit.

In the main, however, the teaching of the Manchester school tended both in external and in internal affairs to a restricted view of the function of government. Government had to maintain order, to restrain men from violence and fraud, to hold them secure in person and property against foreign and domestic enemies, to give them redress against injury, that so they may rely on reaping where they have sown, may enjoy the fruits of their industry, may enter unimpeded into what arrangements they will with one another for their mutual benefit. Let us see what criticism was passed on this view by the contemporaries of Cobden and by the loud voice of the facts themselves. The old economic régime had been in decay throughout the eighteenth century. The divorce of the labourer from the land was complete at the time when the Anti-Corn Law League was formed. The mass of the English peasantry were landless labourers working for a weekly wage of about ten or twelve shillings, and often for a good deal less. The rise of machine industry since 1760 had destroyed the old domestic system and reduced the operative in the towns to the position of a factory hand under an employer, who found the road to wealth easy in the monopoly of manufacture enjoyed by this country for two generations after the Napoleonic war. The factory system early brought matters to a head at one point by the systematic employment of women and young children under conditions which outraged the public conscience when they became known. In the case of children it was admitted from an early date, it was urged by Cobden himself, that the principle of free contract could not apply. Admitting, for the sake of argument, that the adult could make a better bargain for himself or herself than any one could do for him or her, no one could contend that the pauper child apprenticed by Poor Law guardians to a manufacturer had any say or could have any judgment as to the work which it was set to do. It had to be protected, and experience showed that it had to be protected by law. Free contract did not solve the question of the helpless child. It left it to be "exploited" by the employer in his own interest, and whatever regard might be shown for its health and well-being by individuals was a matter of individual benevolence, not a right secured by the necessary operation of the system of liberty.

But these arguments admitted of great extension. If the child was helpless, was the grown-up person, man or woman, in a much better position? Here was the owner of a mill employing five hundred hands. Here was an operative possessed of no alternative means of subsistence seeking employment. Suppose them to bargain as to terms. If the bargain failed, the employer lost one man and had four hundred and ninety-nine to keep his mill going. At worst he might for a day or two, until another operative appeared, have a little difficulty in working a single machine. During the same days the operative might have nothing to eat, and might see his children going hungry. Where was the effective liberty in such an arrangement? The operatives themselves speedily found that there was none, and had from an early period in the rise of the machine industry sought to redress the balance by combination. Now, combination was naturally disliked by employers, and it was strongly suspect to believers in liberty because it put constraint upon individuals. Yet trade unions gained the first step in emancipation through the action of Place and the Radicals in 1824, more perhaps because these men conceived trade unions as the response of labour to oppressive laws which true freedom of competition would render superfluous than because they founded any serious hopes of permanent social progress upon Trade Unionism itself. In point of fact, the critical attitude was not without its justification. Trade Unionism can be protective in spirit and oppressive in action. Nevertheless, it was essential to the maintenance of their industrial standard by the artisan classes, because it alone, in the absence of drastic legislative protection, could do something to redress the inequality between employer and employed. It gave, upon the whole, far more freedom to the workman than it took away, and in this we learn an important lesson which has far wider application. In the matter of contract true freedom postulates substantial equality between the parties. In proportion as one party is in a position of vantage, he is able to dictate his terms. In proportion as the other party is in a weak position, he must accept unfavourable terms. Hence the truth of Walker's dictum that economic injuries tend to perpetuate themselves. The more a class is brought low, the greater its difficulty in rising again without assistance. For purposes of legislation the State has been exceedingly slow to accept this view. It began, as we saw, with the child, where the case was overwhelming. It went on to include the "young person" and the woman—not without criticism from those who held by woman's rights, and saw in this extension of tutelage an enlargement of male domination. Be that as it may, public opinion was brought to this point by the belief that it was intervening in an exceptional manner to protect a definite class not strong enough to bargain for itself. It drew the line at the adult male; and it is only within our own time, and as the result of a controversy waged for many years within the trade union world itself, that legislation has avowedly undertaken the task of controlling the conditions of industry, the hours, and at length, through the institution of Wages Boards in "sweated industries," the actual remuneration of working people without limitation of age or sex. To this it has been driven by the manifest teaching of experience that liberty without equality is a name of noble sound and squalid result.

In place of the system of unfettered agreements between individual and individual which the school of Cobden contemplated, the industrial system which has actually grown up and is in process of further development rests on conditions prescribed by the State, and within the limits of those conditions is very largely governed by collective arrangements between associations of employers and employed. The law provides for the safety of the worker and the sanitary conditions of employment. It prescribes the length of the working day for women and children in factories and workshops, and for men in mines and on railways.[8] In the future it will probably deal freely with the hours of men. It enables wages boards to establish a legal minimum wage in scheduled industries which will undoubtedly grow in number. It makes employers liable for all injuries suffered by operatives in the course of their employment, and forbids any one to "contract out" of this obligation. Within these limits, it allows freedom of contract. But at this point, in the more highly developed trades, the work is taken up by voluntary associations. Combinations of men have been met by combinations of employers, and wages, hours, and all the details of the industrial bargain are settled by collective agreement through the agency of a joint board with an impartial chairman or referee in case of necessity for an entire locality and even an entire trade. So far have we gone from the free competition of isolated individuals.

This development is sometimes held to have involved the decay and death of the older Liberalism. It is true that in the beginning factory legislation enjoyed a large measure of Conservative support. It was at that stage in accordance with the best traditions of paternal rule, and it commended itself to the religious convictions of men of whom Lord Shaftesbury was the typical example. It is true, also, that it was bitterly opposed by Cobden and Bright. On the other hand, Radicals like J. Cam Hobhouse took a leading part in the earlier legislation, and Whig Governments passed the very important Acts of 1833 and 1847. The cleavage of opinion, in fact, cut across the ordinary divisions of party. What is more to the purpose is that, as experience ripened, the implications of the new legislation became clearer, and men came to see that by industrial control they were not destroying liberty but confirming it. A new and more concrete conception of liberty arose and many old presuppositions were challenged.

Let us look for a moment at these presuppositions. We have seen that the theory of *laissez-faire* assumed that the State would hold the ring. That is to say, it would suppress force and fraud, keep property safe, and aid men in enforcing contracts. On these conditions, it was maintained, men should be absolutely free to compete with one another, so that their best energies should be called forth, so that each should feel himself responsible for the guidance of his own life, and exert his manhood to the utmost. But why, it might be asked, on these

---

[8] Indirectly it has for long limited the hours of men in factories owing to the interdependence of the adult male with the female and child operative.

conditions, just these and no others? Why should the State ensure protection of person and property? The time was when the strong man armed kept his goods, and incidentally his neighbour's goods too if he could get hold of them. Why should the State intervene to do for a man that which his ancestor did for himself? Why should a man who has been soundly beaten in physical fight go to a public authority for redress? How much more manly to fight his own battle! Was it not a kind of pauperization to make men secure in person and property through no efforts of their own, by the agency of a state machinery operating over their heads? Would not a really consistent individualism abolish this machinery? "But," the advocate of *laissez-faire* may reply, "the use of force is criminal, and the State must suppress crime." So men held in the nineteenth century. But there was an earlier time when they did not take this view, but left it to individuals and their kinsfolk to revenge their own injuries by their own might. Was not this a time of more unrestricted individual liberty? Yet the nineteenth century regarded it, and justly, as an age of barbarism. What, we may ask in our turn, is the essence of crime? May we not say that any intentional injury to another may be legitimately punished by a public authority, and may we not say that to impose twelve hours' daily labour on a child was to inflict a greater injury than the theft of a purse for which a century ago a man might be hanged? On what principle, then, is the line drawn, so as to specify certain injuries which the State may prohibit and to mark off others which it must leave untouched? Well, it may be said, *volenti non fit injuria.* No wrong is done to a man by a bargain to which he is a willing party. That may be, though there are doubtful cases. But in the field that has been in question the contention is that one party is not willing. The bargain is a forced bargain. The weaker man consents as one slipping over a precipice might consent to give all his fortune to one who will throw him a rope on no other terms. This is not true consent. True consent is free consent, and full freedom of consent implies equality on the part of both parties to the bargain. Just as government first secured the elements of freedom for all when it prevented the physically stronger man from slaying, beating, despoiling his neighbours, so it secures a larger measure of freedom for all by every restriction which it imposes with a view to preventing one man from making use of any of his advantages to the disadvantage of others.

There emerges a distinction between unsocial and social freedom. Unsocial freedom is the right of a man to use his powers without regard to the wishes or interests of any one but himself. Such freedom is theoretically possible for an individual. It is antithetic to all public control. It is theoretically impossible for a plurality of individuals living in mutual contact. Socially it is a contradiction, unless the desires of all men were automatically attuned to social ends. Social freedom, then, for any epoch short of the millennium rests on restraint. It is a freedom that can be enjoyed by all the members of a community, and it is the freedom to choose among those lines of activity which do not involve injury to others. As experience of the social effects of action ripens, and as the social conscience is awakened, the conception of injury is widened and insight into its causes is deepened. The area of restraint is therefore increased. But, inasmuch as injury inflicted is itself crippling to the sufferer, as it lowers his health, confines his life, cramps his powers, so the prevention of such injury sets him free. The restraint of the aggressor is the freedom of the sufferer, and only by restraint on the actions by which men injure one another do they as a whole community gain freedom in all courses of conduct that can be pursued without ultimate social disharmony.

It is, therefore, a very shallow wit that taunts contemporary Liberalism with inconsistency in opposing economic protection while it supports protective legislation for the manual labourer. The two things have nothing in common but that they are restraints intended to operate in the interests of somebody. The one is a restraint which, in the Liberal view, would operate in favour of certain industries and interests to the prejudice of others, and, on the whole, in favour of those who are already more fortunately placed and against the poorer classes. The other is a restraint conceived in the interest primarily of the poorer classes with the object of securing to them a more effective freedom and a nearer approach to equality of conditions in industrial relations. There is point in the argument only for those who conceive liberty as opposed to restraint as such. For those who understand that all social liberty rests upon restraint, that restraint of one man in one respect is the condition of the freedom of other men in that respect, the taunt has no meaning whatever. The liberty which is good is not the liberty of one gained at the expense of others, but the liberty which can be enjoyed by all who dwell together, and this liberty depends on and is measured by the completeness with which by law, custom, or their own feelings they are restrained from mutual injury.

Individualism, as ordinarily understood, not only takes the policeman and the law court for granted. It also takes the rights of property for granted. But what is meant by the rights of property? In ordinary use the phrase means just that system to which long usage has accustomed us. This is a system under which a man is free to acquire by any method of production or exchange within the limits of the law whatever he can of land, consumable goods, or capital; to dispose of it at his own will and pleasure for his own purposes, to destroy it if he likes, to give it away or sell it as it suits him, and at death to bequeath it to whomsoever he will. The State, it is admitted, can take a part of a man's property by taxation. For the State is a necessity, and men must pay a price for security; but in all taxation the State on this view is taking something from a man which is "his," and in so doing is justified only by necessity. It has no "right" to deprive the individual of anything that is his in order to promote objects of its own which are not necessary to the common order. To do so is to infringe individual rights and make a man contribute by force to objects which he may view with indifference or even with dislike. "Socialistic" taxation is an infringement of individual freedom, the freedom to hold one's own and do as one will with one's own. Such seems to be the ordinary view.

But a consistent theory of liberty could not rest wholly satisfied with the actual system under which property is held. The first point of attack, already pressed by the disciples of Cobden, was the barrier to free exchange in the matter of land. It was not and still is not easy for the landless to acquire land, and in the name of free contract Cobden and his disciples pressed for cheap and unimpeded transfer. But a more searching criticism was possible. Land is limited in amount, certain kinds of land very narrowly limited. Where there is limitation of supply monopoly is always possible, and against monopoly the principles of free competition declared war. To Cobden himself, free trade in land was the pendant to free trade in goods. But the attack on the land monopoly could be carried much further, and might lead the individualist who was in earnest about his principles to march a certain distance on parallel lines with the Socialist enemy. This has, in fact, occurred in the school of Henry George. This school holds by competition, but by competition only on the basis of a genuine freedom and equality for all individuals. To secure this basis, it would purge the social system of all elements of monopoly, of which the private ownership of land is in its view the most important. This object, it maintains, can be secured only through the absorption by the State of all elements of monopoly value. Now, monopoly value accrues whenever anything of worth to men of which the supply is limited falls into private hands. In this case competition fails. There is no check upon the owner except the limitations of demand. He can exact a price which bears no necessary relation to the cost of any effort of his own. In addition to normal wages and profits, he can extract from the necessities of others a surplus, to which the name of economic rent is given. He can also hold up his property and refuse to allow others to make use of it until the time when its full value has accrued, thereby increasing the rent which he will ultimately receive at the cost of much loss in the interim to society.

Monopolies in our country fall into three classes. There is, first, the monopoly of land. Urban rents, for example, represent not merely the cost of building, nor the cost of building plus the site, as it would be if sites of the kind required were unlimited in amount. They represent the cost of a site where the supply falls short of the demand, that is to say, where there is an element of monopoly. And site value—the element in the actual cost of a house or factory that depends on its position—varies directly with the degree of this monopoly. This value the land nationalizer contends is not created by the owner. It is created by society. In part it is due to the general growth of the country to which the increase of population and the rise of town life is to be attributed. In part it depends on the growth of the particular locality, and in part on the direct expenditure of the ratepayers' money in sanitation and other improvements which make the place one where people can live and industry can thrive. Directly and indirectly, the community creates the site value. The landlord receives it, and, receiving it, can charge any one who wants to live or carry on industry upon the site with rent to the full amount. The land-nationalizer, looking at rights of property purely from the point of view of the individual, denies the justice of this arrangement, and he sees no solution except this—that the monopoly value should pass back to the community which creates it. Accordingly, he favours the taxation of site value to its full amount. Another element of monopoly arises from industries in which competition is inapplicable—the supply of gas and water, for example, a tramway service, and in some conditions a railway service. Here competition may be wasteful if not altogether impossible; and here again, on the lines of a strictly consistent individualism, if the industry is allowed to fall into private hands the owners will be able to secure something more than the normal profits of competitive industry. They will profit by monopoly at the expense of the general consumer, and the remedy is public control or public ownership. The latter is the more complete and efficacious remedy, and it is also the remedy of municipal socialism. Lastly, there may be forms of monopoly created by the State, such as the sale of liquor as restricted by the licensing system. In accordance with competitive ideas the value so created ought not to pass into private hands, and if on social grounds the monopoly is maintained, the taxation of licensed premises ought to be so arranged that the monopoly value returns to the community.

Up to this point a thoroughly consistent individualism can work in harmony with socialism, and it is this partial alliance which has, in fact, laid down the lines of later Liberal finance. The great Budget of 1909 had behind it the united forces of Socialist and individualist opinion. It may be added that there is a fourth form of monopoly which would be open to the same double attack, but it is one of which less has been heard in Great Britain than in the United States. It is possible under a competitive system for rivals to come to an agreement. The more powerful may coerce the weaker, or a number of equals may agree to work together. Thus competition may defeat itself, and industry may be marshalled into trusts or other combinations for the private advantage against the public interest. Such combinations, predicted by Karl Marx as the appointed means of dissolving the competitive system, have been kept at bay in this country by Free Trade. Under Protection they constitute the most urgent problem of the day. Even here the railways, to take one example, are rapidly moving to a system of combination, the economies of which are obvious, while its immediate result is monopoly, and its assured end is nationalization.

Thus individualism, when it grapples with the facts, is driven no small distance along Socialist lines. Once again we have found that to maintain individual freedom and equality we have to extend the sphere of social control. But to carry through the real principles of Liberalism, to achieve social liberty and living equality of rights, we shall have to probe still deeper. We must not assume any of the rights of property as axiomatic. We must look at their actual working and consider how they affect the life of society. We shall have to ask whether, if we could abolish all monopoly on articles of limited supply, we should yet have dealt with all the causes that contribute to social injustice and industrial disorder, whether we should have rescued the sweated worker, afforded to every man adequate security for a fair return for an honest day's toil, and prevented the use of economic advantage to procure gain for one man at the expense of another. We should have to ask whether we had the basis of a just delimitation between the rights of the community and those of the individual, and therewith a due appreciation of the appropriate ends of the State and the equitable basis of taxation. These inquiries take us to first principles, and to approach that part of our discussion it is desirable to carry further our sketch of the historic development of Liberalism in thought and action.

CHAPTER V

GLADSTONE AND MILL

From the middle of the nineteenth century two great names stand out in the history of British Liberalism—that of Gladstone in the world of action, that of Mill in the world of thought. Differing in much, they agreed in one respect. They had the supreme virtue of keeping their minds fresh and open to new ideas, and both of them in consequence advanced to a deeper interpretation of social life as they grew older. In 1846 Gladstone ranked as a Conservative, but he parted from his old traditions under the leadership of Peel on the question of Free Trade, and for many years to come the most notable of his public services lay in the completion of the Cobdenite policy of financial emancipation. In the pursuit of this policy he was brought into collision with the House of Lords, and it was his active intervention in 1859-60 which saved the Commons from a humiliating surrender, and secured its financial supremacy unimpaired until 1909. In the following decade he stood for the extension of the suffrage, and it was his Government which, in 1884, carried the extension of the representative principle to the point at which it rested twenty-seven years later. In economics Gladstone kept upon the whole to the Cobdenite principles which he acquired in middle life. He was not sympathetically disposed to the "New Unionism" and the semi-socialistic ideas that came at the end of the 'eighties, which, in fact, constituted a powerful cross current to the political work that he had immediately in hand. Yet in relation to Irish land he entered upon a new departure which threw over freedom of contract in a leading case where the two parties were on glaringly unequal terms. No abstract thinker, he had a passion for justice in the concrete which was capable of carrying him far. He knew tyranny when he saw it, and upon it he waged unremitting and many-sided war.

But his most original work was done in the sphere of imperial relations. The maligned Majuba settlement was an act of justice which came too late to effect a permanent undoing of mischief. All the greater was the courage of the statesman who could throw himself at that time upon the inherent force of national liberty and international fair dealing. In the case of Ireland Gladstone again relied on the same principles, but another force was necessary to carry the day, a force which no man can command, the force of time. In international dealings generally Gladstone was a pioneer. His principle was not precisely that of Cobden. He was not a non-interventionist. He took action on behalf of Greece, and would have done so on behalf of the Armenians, to save the national honour and prevent a monstrous wrong. The Gladstonian principle may be defined by antithesis to that of Machiavelli, and to that of Bismarck, and to the practice of every Foreign Office. As that practice proceeds on the principle that reasons of State justify everything, so Gladstone proceeded on the principle that reasons of State justify nothing that is not justified already by the human conscience. The statesman is for him a man charged with maintaining not only the material interests but the honour of his country. He is a citizen of the world in that he represents his nation, which is a member of the community of the world. He has to recognize rights and duties, as every representative of every other human organization has to recognize rights and duties. There is no line drawn beyond which human obligations cease. There is no gulf across which the voice of human suffering cannot be heard, beyond which massacre and torture cease to be execrable. Simply as a patriot, again, a man should recognize that a nation may become great not merely by painting the map red, or extending her commerce beyond all precedent, but also as the champion of justice, the succourer of the oppressed, the established home of freedom. From the denunciation of the Opium War, from the exposure of the Neapolitan prisons, to his last appearance on the morrow of the Constantinople massacre this was the message which Gladstone sought to convey. He was before his time. He was not always able to maintain his principle in his own Cabinet, and on his retirement the world appeared to relapse definitely into the older ways. His own party gave itself up in large measure to opposite views. On the other hand, careful and unprejudiced criticism will recognize that the chief opponent of his old age, Lord Salisbury, had imbibed something of his spirit, and under its influence did much to save the country from the excesses of Imperialism, while his follower, Sir Henry Campbell-Bannerman, used the brief term of his power to reverse the policy of racial domination in South Africa and to prove the value of the old Gladstonian trust in the recuperative force of political freedom. It may be added that, if cynicism has since appeared to hold the field in international politics, it is the cynicism of terror rather than the cynicism of ambition. The Scare has superseded the Vision as the moving force in our external relations, and there are now signs that the Scare in turn has spent its force and is making room at last for Sense.

In other respects, Gladstone was a moral rather than an intellectual force. He raised the whole level of public life. By habitually calling upon what was best in men, he deepened the sense of public responsibility and paved the way, half unconsciously, for the fuller exercise of the social conscience. Mill was also a moral force, and the most persistent influence of his books is more an effect of character than of intellect. But, in place of Gladstone's driving power and practical capacity, Mill had the qualities of a life-long learner, and in his single person he spans the interval between the old and the new Liberalism. Brought up on the pure milk of the Benthamite word, he never definitely abandoned the first principles of his father. But he was perpetually bringing them into contact with fresh experience and new trains of thought, considering how they worked, and how they ought to be modified in order to maintain what was really sound and valuable in their content. Hence, Mill is the easiest person in the world to convict of inconsistency, incompleteness, and lack of rounded system. Hence, also, his work will survive the death of many consistent, complete, and perfectly rounded systems.

As a utilitarian, Mill cannot appeal to any rights of the individual that can be set in opposition to the public welfare. His method is to show that the permanent welfare of the public is bound up with the rights of the individual. Of course, there are occasions on which the immediate expediency of the public would be met by ignoring personal rights. But if the rule of expediency were followed there would be neither right nor law at all. There would be no fixed rules in social life, and nothing to which men could trust in guiding their conduct. For the utilitarian, then, the question of right resolves itself into the question: What claim is it, in general and as a matter of principle, advisable for society to recognize? What in any given relation are the permanent conditions of social health? In regard to liberty Mill's reply turns on the moral or spiritual forces which determine the life of society. First, particularly as regards freedom of thought and discussion, society needs light. Truth has a social value, and we are never to suppose that we are in the possession of complete and final truth. But truth is only to be sought by experience in the world of thought, and of action as well. In the process of experimentation there are endless opportunities of error, and the free search for truth therefore involves friction and waste. The promulgation of error will do harm, a harm that might be averted if error were suppressed. But suppression by any other means than those of rational suasion is one of those remedies which cure the disease by killing the patient. It paralyzes the free search for truth. Not only so, but there is an element of positive value in honest error which places it above mechanically accepted truth. So far as it is honest it springs from the spontaneous operation of the mind on the basis of some partial and incomplete experience. It is, so far as it goes, an interpretation of experience, though a faulty one, whereas the belief imposed by authority is no interpretation of experience at all. It involves no personal effort. Its blind acceptance seals the resignation of the will and the intellect to effacement and stultification.

The argument on this side does not rest on human fallibility. It appeals in its full strength to those who are most confident that they possess truth final and complete. They are asked to recognize that the way in which this truth must be communicated to others is not by material but by spiritual means, and that if they hold out physical threats as a deterrent, or worldly advantage as a means of persuasion, they are destroying not merely the fruits but the very root of truth as it grows within the human mind. Yet the argument receives additional force when we consider the actual history of human belief. The candid man who knows anything of the movements of thought will recognize that even the faith which is most vital to him is something that has grown through the generations, and he may infer, if he is reasonable, that as it has grown in the past so, if it has the vital seed within it, it will grow in the future. It may be permanent in outline, but in content it will change. But, if truth itself is an expanding circle of ideas that grows through criticism and by modification, we need say no more as to the rough and imperfect apprehension of truth which constitutes the dominant opinion of society at any given moment. It needs little effort of detachment to appreciate the danger of any limitation of inquiry by the collective will whether its organ be law or the repressive force of public opinion.

The foundation of liberty on this side, then, is the conception of thought as a growth dependent on spiritual laws, flourishing in the movement of ideas as guided by experience, reflection and feeling, corrupted by the intrusion of material considerations, slain by the guillotine of finality. The same conception is broadened out to cover the whole idea of personality. Social well-being cannot be incompatible with individual well-being. But individual well-being has as its foundation the responsible life of the rational creature. Manhood, and Mill would emphatically add womanhood too, rests on the spontaneous development of faculty. To find vent for the capacities of feeling, of emotion, of thought, of action, is to find oneself. The result is no anarchy. The self so found has as the pivot of its life the power of control. To introduce some unity into life, some harmony into thought, action and feeling, is its central achievement, and to realize its relation to others and guide its own life thereby, its noblest rule. But the essential of control is that it should be self-control. Compulsion may be necessary for the purposes of external order, but it adds nothing to the inward life that is the true being of man. It even threatens it with loss of authority and infringes the sphere of its responsibility. It is a means and not an end, and a means that readily becomes a danger to ends that are very vital. Under self-guidance individuals will diverge widely, and some of their eccentricities will be futile, others wasteful, others even painful and abhorrent to witness. But, upon the whole, it is good that they should differ. Individuality is an element of well-being, and that not only because it is the necessary consequence of self-government, but because, after all allowances for waste, the common life is fuller and richer for the multiplicity of types that it includes, and that go to enlarge the area of collective experience. The larger wrong done by the repression of women is not the loss to women themselves who constitute one half of the community, but the impoverishment of the community as a whole, the loss of all the elements in the common stock which the free play of the woman's mind would contribute.

Similar principles underlie Mill's treatment of representative government. If the adult citizen, male or female, has a right to vote, it is not so much as a means to the enforcement of his claims upon society, but rather as a means of enforcing his personal responsibility for the actions of the community. The problem of character is the determining issue in the question of government. If men could be spoon-fed with happiness, a benevolent despotism would be the ideal system. If they are to take a part in working out their own salvation, they must be summoned to their share in the task of directing the common life. Carrying this principle further, Mill turned the edge of the common objection to the extension of the suffrage based on the ignorance and the irresponsibility of the voters. To learn anything men must practise. They must be trusted with more responsibility if they are to acquire the sense of responsibility. There were dangers in the process, but there were greater dangers and there were fewer elements of hope as long as the mass of the population was left outside the circle of civic rights and duties. The greatest danger that Mill saw in democracy was that of the tyranny of the majority. He emphasized, perhaps more than any Liberal teacher before him, the difference between the desire of the majority and the good of the community. He recognized that the different rights for which the Liberal was wont to plead might turn out in practice hard to reconcile with one another, that if personal liberty were fundamental it might only be imperilled by a so-called political liberty which would give to the majority unlimited powers of coercion. He was, therefore, for many years anxiously concerned with the means of securing a fair hearing and fair representation to minorities, and as a pioneer of the movement for Proportional Representation he sought to make Parliament the reflection not of a portion of the people, however preponderant numerically, but of the whole.

On the economic side of social life Mill recognized in principle the necessity of controlling contract where the parties were not on equal terms, but his insistence on personal responsibility made him chary in extending the principle to grown-up persons, and his especial attachment to the cause of feminine emancipation led him to resist the tide of feeling which was, in fact, securing the first elements of emancipation for the woman worker. He trusted at the outset of his career to the elevation of the standard of comfort as the best means of improving the position of the wage-earner, and in this elevation he regarded the limitation of the family as an essential condition. As he advanced in life, however, he became more and more dissatisfied with the whole structure of a system which left the mass of the population in the position of wage-earners, while the minority lived on rents, profits, and the interest on invested capital. He came to look forward to a co-operative organization of society in which a man would learn to "dig and weave for his country," as he now is prepared to fight for it, and in which the surplus products of industry would be distributed among the producers. In middle life voluntary co-operation appeared to him the best means to this end, but towards the close he recognized that his change of views was such as, on the whole, to rank him with the Socialists, and the brief exposition of the Socialist ideal given in his Autobiography remains perhaps the best summary statement of Liberal Socialism that we possess.

CHAPTER VI

THE HEART OF LIBERALISM

The teaching of Mill brings us close to the heart of Liberalism. We learn from him, in the first place, that liberty is no mere formula of law, or of the restriction of law. There may be a tyranny of custom, a tyranny of opinion, even a tyranny of circumstance, as real as any tyranny of government and more pervasive. Nor does liberty rest on the self-assertion of the individual. There is scope abundant for Liberalism and illiberalism in personal conduct. Nor is liberty opposed to discipline, to organization, to strenuous conviction as to what is true and just. Nor is it to be identified with tolerance of opposed opinions. The Liberal does not meet opinions which he conceives to be false with toleration, as though they did not matter. He meets them with justice, and exacts for them a fair hearing as though they mattered just as much as his own. He is always ready to put his own convictions to the proof, not because he doubts them, but because he believes in them. For, both as to that which he holds for true and as to that which he holds for false, he believes that one final test applies. Let error have free play, and one of two things will happen. Either as it develops, as its implications and consequences become clear, some elements of truth will appear within it. They will separate themselves out; they will go to enrich the stock of human ideas; they will add something to the truth which he himself mistakenly took as final; they will serve to explain the root of the error; for error itself is generally a truth misconceived, and it is only when it is explained that it is finally and satisfactorily confuted. Or, in the alternative, no element of truth will appear. In that case the more fully the error is understood, the more patiently it is followed up in all the windings of its implications and consequences, the more thoroughly will it refute itself. The cancerous growth cannot be extirpated by the knife. The root is always left, and it is only the evolution of the self-protecting anti-toxin that works the final cure. Exactly parallel is the logic of truth. The more the truth is developed in all its implications, the greater is the opportunity of detecting any element of error that it may contain; and, conversely, if no error appears, the more completely does it establish itself as the whole truth and nothing but the truth. Liberalism applies the wisdom of Gamaliel in no spirit of indifference, but in the full conviction of the potency of truth. If this thing be of man, *i. e.* if it is not rooted in actual verity, it will come to nought. If it be of God, let us take care that we be not found fighting against God.

Divergences of opinion, of character, of conduct are not unimportant matters. They may be most serious matters, and no one is called on in the name of Liberalism to overlook their seriousness. There are, for example, certain disqualifications inherent in the profession of certain opinions. It is not illiberal to recognize such disqualifications. It is not illiberal for a Protestant in choosing a tutor for his son to reject a conscientious Roman Catholic who avows that all his teaching is centred on the doctrine of his Church. It would be illiberal to reject the same man for the specific purpose of teaching arithmetic, if he avowed that he had no intention of using his position for the purpose of religious propagandism. For the former purpose the divergence of religious opinion is an inherent disqualification. It negates the object propounded, which is the general education of the boy on lines in which the father believes. For the latter purpose the opinion is no disqualification. The devout Catholic accepts the multiplication table, and can impart his knowledge without reference to the infallibility of the Pope. To refuse to employ him is to impose an extraneous penalty on his convictions. It is not illiberal for an editor to decline the services of a member of the opposite party as a leader writer, or even as a political reviewer or in any capacity in which his opinions would affect his work. It is illiberal to reject him as a compositor or as a clerk, or in any capacity in which his opinions would not affect his work for the paper. It is not illiberal to refuse a position of trust to the man whose record shows that he is likely to abuse such a trust. It is illiberal— and this the "moralist" has yet to learn—to punish a man who has done a wrong in one relation by excluding him from the performance of useful social functions for which he is perfectly fitted, by which he could at once serve society and re-establish his own self-respect. There may, however, yet come a time when Liberalism, already recognized as a duty in religion and in politics, will take its true place at the centre of our ethical conceptions, and will be seen to have its application not only to him whom we conceive to be the teacher of false opinions, but to the man whom we hold a sinner.

The ground of Liberalism so understood is certainly not the view that a man's personal opinions are socially indifferent, nor that his personal morality matters nothing to others. So far as Mill rested his case on the distinction between self-regarding actions and actions that affect others, he was still dominated by the older individualism. We should frankly recognize that there is no side of a man's life which is unimportant to society, for whatever he is, does, or thinks may affect his own well-being, which is and ought to be matter of common concern, and may also directly or indirectly affect the thought, action, and character of those with whom he comes in contact. The underlying principle may be put in two ways. In the first place, the man is much more than his opinions and his actions. Carlyle and Sterling did not differ "except in opinion." To most of us that is just what difference means. Carlyle was aware that there was something much deeper, something that opinion just crassly formulates, and for the most part formulates inadequately, that is the real man. The real man is something more than is ever adequately expressed in terms which his fellows can understand; and just as his essential humanity lies deeper than all distinctions of rank, and class, and colour, and even, though in a different sense, of sex, so also it goes far below those comparatively external events which make one man figure as a saint and another as a criminal. This sense of ultimate oneness is the real meaning of equality, as it is the foundation of social solidarity and the bond which, if genuinely experienced, resists the disruptive force of all conflict, intellectual, religious, and ethical.

But, further, while personal opinions and social institutions are like crystallized results, achievements that have been won by certain definite processes of individual or collective effort, human personality is that within which lives and grows, which can be destroyed but cannot be made, which cannot be taken to pieces and repaired, but can be placed under conditions in which it will flourish and expand, or, if it is diseased, under conditions in which it will heal itself by its own recuperative powers. The foundation of liberty is the idea of growth. Life is learning, but whether in theory or practice what a man genuinely learns is what he absorbs, and what he absorbs depends on the energy which he himself puts forth in response to his surroundings. Thus, to come at once to the real crux, the question of moral discipline, it is of course possible to reduce a man to order and prevent him from being a nuisance to his neighbours by arbitrary control and harsh punishment. This may be to the comfort of the neighbours, as is admitted, but regarded as a moral discipline it is a contradiction in terms. It is doing less than nothing for the character of the man himself. It is merely crushing him, and unless his will is killed the effect will be seen if ever the superincumbent pressure is by chance removed. It is also possible, though it takes a much higher skill, to teach the same man to discipline himself, and this is to foster the development of will, of personality, of self control, or whatever we please to call that central harmonizing power which makes us capable of directing our own lives. Liberalism is the belief that society can safely be founded on this self-directing power of personality, that it is only on this foundation that a true community can be built, and that so established its foundations are so deep and so wide that there is no limit that we can place to the extent of the building. Liberty then becomes not so much a right of the individual as a necessity of society. It rests not on the claim of A to be let alone by B, but on the duty of B to treat A as a rational being. It is not right to let crime alone or to let error alone, but it is imperative to treat the criminal or the mistaken or the ignorant as beings capable of right and truth, and to lead them on instead of merely beating them down. The rule of liberty is just the application of rational method. It is the opening of the door to the appeal of reason, of imagination, of social feeling; and except through the response to this appeal there is no assured progress of society.

Now, I am not contending that these principles are free from difficulty in application. At many points they suggest difficulties both in theory and in practice, with some of which I shall try to deal later on. Nor, again, am I contending that freedom is the universal solvent, or the idea of liberty the sole foundation on which a true social philosophy can be based. On the contrary, freedom is only one side of social life. Mutual aid is not less important than mutual forbearance, the theory of collective action no less fundamental than the theory of personal freedom. But, in an inquiry where all the elements are so closely interwoven as they are in the field of social life, the point of departure becomes almost indifferent. Wherever we start we shall, if we are quite frank and consistent, be led on to look at the whole from some central point, and this, I think, has happened to us in working with the conception of 'liberty.' For, beginning with the right of the individual, and the antithesis between personal freedom and social control, we have been led on to a point at which we regard liberty as primarily a matter of social interest, as something flowing from the necessities of continuous advance in those regions of truth and of ethics which constitute the matters of highest social concern. At the same time, we have come to look for the effect of liberty in the firmer establishment of social solidarity, as the only foundation on which such solidarity can securely rest. We have, in fact, arrived by a path of our own at that which is ordinarily described as the organic conception of the relation between the individual and society—a conception towards which Mill worked through his career, and which forms the starting-point of T. H. Green's philosophy alike in ethics and in politics.

The term organic is so much used and abused that it is best to state simply what it means. A thing is called organic when it is made up of parts which are quite distinct from one another, but which are destroyed or vitally altered when they are removed from the whole. Thus, the human body is organic because its life depends on the functions performed by many organs, while each of these organs depends in turn on the life of the body, perishing and decomposing if removed therefrom. Now, the organic view of society is equally simple. It means that, while the life of society is nothing but the life of individuals as they act one upon another, the life of the individual in turn would be something utterly different if he could be separated from society. A great deal of him would not exist at all. Even if he himself could maintain physical existence by the luck and skill of a Robinson Crusoe, his mental and moral being would, if it existed at all, be something quite different from anything that we know. By language, by training, by simply living with others, each of us absorbs into his system the social atmosphere that surrounds us. In particular, in the matter of rights and duties which is cardinal for Liberal theory, the relation of the individual to the community is everything. His rights and his duties are alike defined by the common good. What, for example, is my right? On the face of it, it is something that I claim. But a mere claim is nothing. I might claim anything and everything. If my claim is of right it is because it is sound, well grounded, in the judgment of an impartial observer. But an impartial observer will not consider me alone. He will equally weigh the opposed claims of others. He will take us in relation to one another, that is to say, as individuals involved in a social relationship. Further, if his decision is in any sense a rational one, it must rest on a principle of some kind; and again, as a rational man, any principle which he asserts he must found on some good result which it serves or embodies, and as an impartial man he must take the good of every one affected into account. That is to say, he must found his judgment on the common good. An individual right, then, cannot conflict with the common good, nor could any right exist apart from the common good.

The argument might seem to make the individual too subservient to society. But this is to forget the other side of the original supposition. Society consists wholly of persons. It has no distinct personality separate from and superior to those of its members. It has, indeed, a certain collective life and character. The

British nation is a unity with a life of its own. But the unity is constituted by certain ties that bind together all British subjects, which ties are in the last resort feelings and ideas, sentiments of patriotism, of kinship, a common pride, and a thousand more subtle sentiments that bind together men who speak a common language, have behind them a common history, and understand one another as they can understand no one else. The British nation is not a mysterious entity over and above the forty odd millions of living souls who dwell together under a common law. Its life is their life, its well-being or ill-fortune their well-being or ill-fortune. Thus, the common good to which each man's rights are subordinate is a good in which each man has a share. This share consists in realizing his capacities of feeling, of loving, of mental and physical energy, and in realizing these he plays his part in the social life, or, in Green's phrase, he finds his own good in the common good.

Now, this phrase, it must be admitted, involves a certain assumption, which may be regarded as the fundamental postulate of the organic view of society. It implies that such a fulfilment or full development of personality is practically possible not for one man only but for all members of a community. There must be a line of development open along which each can move in harmony with others. Harmony in the full sense would involve not merely absence of conflict but actual support. There must be for each, then, possibilities of development such as not merely to permit but actively to further the development of others. Now, the older economists conceived a natural harmony, such that the interests of each would, if properly understood and unchecked by outside interference, inevitably lead him in courses profitable to others and to society at large. We saw that this assumption was too optimistic. The conception which we have now reached does not assume so much. It postulates, not that there is an actually existing harmony requiring nothing but prudence and coolness of judgment for its effective operation, but only that there is a possible ethical harmony, to which, partly by discipline, partly by the improvement of the conditions of life, men might attain, and that in such attainment lies the social ideal. To attempt the systematic proof of this postulate would take us into the field of philosophical first principles. It is the point at which the philosophy of politics comes into contact with that of ethics. It must suffice to say here that, just as the endeavour to establish coherent system in the world of thought is the characteristic of the rational impulse which lies at the root of science and philosophy, so the impulse to establish harmony in the world of feeling and action—a harmony which must include all those who think and feel—is of the essence of the rational impulse in the world of practice. To move towards harmony is the persistent impulse of the rational being, even if the goal lies always beyond the reach of accomplished effort.

These principles may appear very abstract, remote from practical life, and valueless for concrete teaching. But this remoteness is of the nature of first principles when taken without the connecting links that bind them to the details of experience. To find some of these links let us take up again our old Liberal principles, and see how they look in the light of the organic, or, as we may now call it, the harmonic conception. We shall readily see, to begin with, that the old idea of equality has its place. For the common good includes every individual. It is founded on personality, and postulates free scope for the development of personality in each member of the community. This is the foundation not only of equal rights before the law, but also of what is called equality of opportunity. It does not necessarily imply actual equality of treatment for all persons any more than it implies original equality of powers.[9] It does, I think, imply that whatever inequality of actual treatment, of income, rank, office, consideration, there be in a good social system, it would rest, not on the interest of the favoured individual as such, but on the common good. If the existence of millionaires on the one hand and of paupers on the other is just, it must be because such contrasts are the result of an economic system which upon the whole works out for the common good, the good of the pauper being included therein as well as the good of the millionaire; that is to say, that when we have well weighed the good and the evil of all parties concerned we can find no alternative open to us which could do better for the good of all. I am not for the moment either attacking or defending any economic system. I point out only that this is the position which according to the organic or harmonic view of society must be made good by any rational defence of grave inequality in the distribution of wealth. In relation to equality, indeed, it appears, oddly enough, that the harmonic principle can adopt wholesale, and even expand, one of the "Rights of Man" as formulated in 1789—"Social distinctions can only be founded upon common utility." If it is really just that A should be superior to B in wealth or power or position, it is only because when the good of all concerned is considered, among whom B is one, it turns out that there is a net gain in the arrangement as compared with any alternative that we can devise.

If we turn from equality to liberty, the general lines of argument have already been indicated, and the discussion of difficulties in detail must be left for the next chapter. It need only be repeated here that on the harmonic principle the fundamental importance of liberty rests on the nature of the "good" itself, and that whether we are thinking of the good of society or the good of the individual. The good is something attained by the development of the basal factors of personality; a development proceeding by the widening of ideas, the awakening of the imagination, the play of affection and passion, the strengthening and extension of rational control. As it is the development of these factors in each human being that makes his life worth having, so it is their harmonious interaction, the response of each to each, that makes of society a living whole. Liberty so interpreted cannot, as we have seen, dispense with restraint; restraint, however, is not an end but a means to an end, and one of the principal elements in that end is the enlargement of liberty.

But the collective activity of the community does not necessarily proceed by coercion or restraint. The more securely it is founded on freedom and general

---

[9] An absurd misconception fostered principally by opponents of equality for controversial purposes.

willing assent, the more it is free to work out all the achievements in which the individual is feeble or powerless while combined action is strong. Human progress, on whatever side we consider it, is found to be in the main social progress, the work of conscious or unconscious co-operation. In this work voluntary association plays a large and increasing part. But the State is one form of association among others, distinguished by its use of coercive power, by its supremacy, and by its claim to control all who dwell within its geographical limits. What the functions of such a form of association are to be we shall have to consider a little further in connection with the other questions which we have already raised. But that, in general, we are justified in regarding the State as one among many forms of human association for the maintenance and improvement of life is the general principle that we have to point out here, and this is the point at which we stand furthest from the older Liberalism. We have, however, already seen some reason for thinking that the older doctrines led, when carefully examined, to a more enlarged conception of State action than appeared on the surface; and we shall see more fully before we have done that the "positive" conception of the State which we have now reached not only involves no conflict with the true principle of personal liberty, but is necessary to its effective realization.

There is, in addition, one principle of historic Liberalism with which our present conception of the State is in full sympathy. The conception of the common good as it has been explained can be realized in its fullness only through the common will. There are, of course, elements of value in the good government of a benevolent despot or of a fatherly aristocracy. Within any peaceful order there is room for many good things to flourish. But the full fruit of social progress is only to be reaped by a society in which the generality of men and women are not only passive recipients but practical contributors. To make the rights and responsibilities of citizens real and living, and to extend them as widely as the conditions of society allow, is thus an integral part of the organic conception of society, and the justification of the democratic principle. It is, at the same time, the justification of nationalism so far as nationalism is founded on a true interpretation of history. For, inasmuch as the true social harmony rests on feeling and makes use of all the natural ties of kinship, of neighbourliness, of congruity of character and belief, and of language and mode of life, the best, healthiest, and most vigorous political unit is that to which men are by their own feelings strongly drawn. Any breach of such unity, whether by forcible disruption or by compulsory inclusion in a larger society of alien sentiments and laws, tends to mutilate—or, at lowest, to cramp—the spontaneous development of social life. National and personal freedom are growths of the same root, and their historic connection rests on no accident, but on ultimate identity of idea.

Thus in the organic conception of society each of the leading ideas of historic Liberalism has its part to play. The ideal society is conceived as a whole which lives and flourishes by the harmonious growth of its parts, each of which in developing on its own lines and in accordance with its own nature tends on the whole to further the development of others. There is some elementary trace of such harmony in every form of social life that can maintain itself, for if the conflicting impulses predominated society would break up, and when they do predominate society does break up. At the other extreme, true harmony is an ideal which it is perhaps beyond the power of man to realize, but which serves to indicate the line of advance. But to admit this is to admit that the lines of possible development for each individual or, to use a more general phrase, for each constituent of the social order are not limited and fixed. There are many possibilities, and the course that will in the end make for social harmony is only one among them, while the possibilities of disharmony and conflict are many. The progress of society like that of the individual depends, then, ultimately on choice. It is not "natural," in the sense in which a physical law is natural, that is, in the sense of going forward automatically from stage to stage without backward turnings, deflections to the left, or fallings away on the right. It is natural only in this sense, that it is the expression of deep-seated forces of human nature which come to their own only by an infinitely slow and cumbersome process of mutual adjustment. Every constructive social doctrine rests on the conception of human progress. The heart of Liberalism is the understanding that progress is not a matter of mechanical contrivance, but of the liberation of living spiritual energy. Good mechanism is that which provides the channels wherein such energy can flow unimpeded, unobstructed by its own exuberance of output, vivifying the social structure, expanding and ennobling the life of mind.

CHAPTER VII

THE STATE AND THE INDIVIDUAL

We have seen something of the principle underlying the Liberal idea and of its various applications. We have now to put the test question. Are these different applications compatible? Will they work together to make that harmonious whole of which it is easy enough to talk in abstract terms? Are they themselves really harmonious in theory and in practice? Does scope for individual development, for example, consort with the idea of equality? Is popular sovereignty a practicable basis of personal freedom, or does it open an avenue to the tyranny of the mob? Will the sentiment of nationality dwell in unison with the ideal of peace? Is the love of liberty compatible with the full realization of the common will? If reconcilable in theory, may not these ideals collide in practice? Are there not clearly occasions demonstrable in history when development in one direction involves retrogression in another? If so, how are we to strike the balance of gain and loss? Does political progress offer us nothing but a choice of evils, or may we have some confidence that, in solving the most pressing problem of the moment, we shall in the end be in a better position for grappling with the obstacles that come next in turn?

I shall deal with these questions as far as limits of space allow, and I will take first the question of liberty and the common will upon which everything turns. Enough has already been said on this topic to enable us to shorten the discussion. We have seen that social liberty rests on restraint. A man can be free to direct his own life only in so far as others are prevented from molesting and interfering with him. So far there is no real departure from the strictest tenets of individualism. We have, indeed, had occasion to examine the application of the doctrine to freedom of contract on the one hand, and to the action of combinations on the other, and have seen reason to think that in either case nominal freedom, that is to say, the absence of legal restraint, might have the effect of impairing real freedom, that is to say, would allow the stronger party to coerce the weaker. We have also seen that the effect of combination may be double edged, that it may restrict freedom on one side and enlarge it on the other. In all these cases our contention has been simply that we should be guided by real and not by verbal considerations,—that we should ask in every case what policy will yield effective freedom—and we have found a close connection in each instance between freedom and equality. In these cases, however, we were dealing with the relations of one man with another, or of one body of men with another, and we could regard the community as an arbiter between them whose business it was to see justice done and prevent the abuse of coercive power. Hence we could treat a very large part of the modern development of social control as motived by the desire for a more effective liberty. The case is not so clear when we find the will of the individual in conflict with the will of the community as a whole. When such conflict occurs, it would seem that we must be prepared for one of two things. Either we must admit the legitimacy of coercion, avowedly not in the interests of freedom but in furtherance, without regard to freedom, of other ends which the community deems good. Or we must admit limitations which may cramp the development of the general will, and perchance prove a serious obstacle to collective progress. Is there any means of avoiding this conflict? Must we leave the question to be fought out in each case by a balance of advantages and disadvantages, or are there any general considerations which help us to determine the true sphere of collective and of private action?

Let us first observe that, as Mill pointed out long ago, there are many forms of collective action which do not involve coercion. The State may provide for certain objects which it deems good without compelling any one to make use of them. Thus it may maintain hospitals, though any one who can pay for them remains free to employ his own doctors and nurses. It may and does maintain a great educational system, while leaving every one free to maintain or to attend a private school. It maintains parks and picture galleries without driving any one into them. There is a municipal tramway service, which does not prevent private people from running motor 'buses along the same streets, and so on. It is true that for the support of these objects rates and taxes are compulsorily levied, but this form of compulsion raises a set of questions of which we shall have to speak in another connection, and does not concern us here. For the moment we have to deal only with those actions of State which compel all citizens, or all whom they concern, to fall in with them and allow of no divergence. This kind of coercion tends to increase. Is its extension necessarily an encroachment upon liberty, or are the elements of value secured by collective control distinct from the elements of value secured by individual choice, so that within due limits each may develop side by side?

We have already declined to solve the problem by applying Mill's distinction between self-regarding and other-regarding actions, first because there are no actions which may not directly or indirectly affect others, secondly because even if there were they would not cease to be matter of concern to others. The common good includes the good of every member of the community, and the injury which a man inflicts upon himself is matter of common concern, even apart from any ulterior effect upon others. If we refrain from coercing a man for his own good, it is not because his good is indifferent to us, but because it cannot be furthered by coercion. The difficulty is founded on the nature of the good itself, which on its personal side depends on the spontaneous flow of feeling checked and guided not by external restraint but by rational self-control. To try to form character by coercion is to destroy it in the making. Personality is not built up from without but grows from within, and the function of the outer order is not to create it, but to provide for it the most suitable conditions of growth. Thus, to the common question whether it is possible to make men good by Act of Parliament, the reply is that it is not possible to compel morality because morality is the act or character of a free agent, but that it is possible to create the conditions under which morality can develop, and among these not the least important is freedom from compulsion by others.

The argument suggests that compulsion is limited not by indifference—how could the character of its members be matter of indifference to the community?—but by its own incapacity to achieve its ends. The spirit cannot be forced. Nor, conversely, can it prevail by force. It may require social expression. It may build up an association, a church for example, to carry out the common objects and maintain the common life of all who are like-minded. But the association must be free, because spiritually everything depends not on what is done but on the will with which it is done. The limit to the value of coercion thus lies not in the restriction of social purpose, but in the conditions of personal life. No force can compel growth. Whatever elements of social value depend on the accord of feeling, on comprehension of meaning, on the assent of will, must come through liberty. Here is the sphere and function of liberty in the social harmony.

Where, then, is the sphere of compulsion, and what is its value? The reply is that compulsion is of value where outward conformity is of value, and this may be in any case where the non-conformity of one wrecks the purpose of others. We have already remarked that liberty itself only rests upon restraint. Thus a religious body is not, properly speaking, free to march in procession through the streets unless people of a different religion are restrained from pelting the procession with stones and pursuing it with insolence. We restrain them from disorder not to teach them the genuine spirit of religion, which they will not learn in the police court, but to secure to the other party the right of worship unmolested. The enforced restraint has its value in the action that it sets free. But we may not only restrain one man from obstructing another—and the extent to which we do this is the measure of the freedom that we maintain—but we may also restrain him from obstructing the general will; and this we have to do whenever uniformity is necessary to the end which the general will has in view. The majority of employers in a trade we may suppose would be willing to adopt certain precautions for the health or safety of their workers, to lower hours or to raise the rate of wages. They are unable to do so, however, as long as a minority, perhaps as long as a single employer, stands out. He would beat them in competition if they were voluntarily to undertake expenses from which he is free. In this case, the will of a minority, possibly the will of one man, thwarts that of the remainder. It coerces them, indirectly, but quite as effectively as if he were their master. If they, by combination, can coerce him no principle of liberty is violated. It is coercion against coercion, differing possibly in form and method, but not in principle or in spirit. Further, if the community as a whole sympathizes with the one side rather than the other, it can reasonably bring the law into play. Its object is not the moral education of the recusant individuals. Its object is to secure certain conditions which it believes necessary for the welfare of its members, and which can only be secured by an enforced uniformity.

It appears, then, that the true distinction is not between self-regarding and other-regarding actions, but between coercive and non-coercive actions. The function of State coercion is to override individual coercion, and, of course, coercion exercised by any association of individuals within the State. It is by this means that it maintains liberty of expression, security of person and property, genuine freedom of contract, the rights of public meeting and association, and finally its own power to carry out common objects undefeated by the recalcitrance of individual members. Undoubtedly it endows both individuals and associations with powers as well as with rights. But over these powers it must exercise supervision in the interests of equal justice. Just as compulsion failed in the sphere of liberty, the sphere of spiritual growth, so liberty fails in the external order wherever, by the mere absence of supervisory restriction, men are able directly or indirectly to put constraint on one another. This is why there is no intrinsic and inevitable conflict between liberty and compulsion, but at bottom a mutual need. The object of compulsion is to secure the most favourable external conditions of inward growth and happiness so far as these conditions depend on combined action and uniform observance. The sphere of liberty is the sphere of growth itself. There is no true opposition between liberty as such and control as such, for every liberty rests on a corresponding act of control. The true opposition is between the control that cramps the personal life and the spiritual order, and the control that is aimed at securing the external and material conditions of their free and unimpeded development.

I do not pretend that this delimitation solves all problems. The "inward" life will seek to express itself in outward acts. A religious ordinance may bid the devout refuse military service, or withhold the payment of a tax, or decline to submit a building to inspection. Here are external matters where conscience and the State come into direct conflict, and where is the court of appeal that is to decide between them? In any given case the right, as judged by the ultimate effect on human welfare, may, of course, be on the one side, or on the other, or between the two. But is there anything to guide the two parties as long as each believes itself to be in the right and sees no ground for waiving its opinion? To begin with, clearly the State does well to avoid such conflicts by substituting alternatives. Other duties than that of military service may be found for a follower of Tolstoy, and as long as he is willing to take his full share of burdens the difficulty is fairly met. Again, the mere convenience of the majority cannot be fairly weighed against the religious convictions of the few. It might be convenient that certain public work should be done on Saturday, but mere convenience would be an insufficient ground for compelling Jews to participate in it. Religious and ethical conviction must be weighed against religious and ethical conviction. It is not number that counts morally, but the belief that is reasoned out according to the best of one's lights as to the necessities of the common good. But the conscience of the community has its rights just as much as the conscience of the individual. If we are convinced that the inspection of a convent laundry is required in the interest, not of mere official routine, but of justice and humanity, we can do nothing but insist upon it, and when all has been done that can be done to save the individual conscience the common conviction of the common good must have its way. In the end the external order belongs to the community, and the right of protest to the individual.

On the other side, the individual owes more to the community than is always recognized. Under modern conditions he is too much inclined to take for granted what the State does for him and to use the personal security and liberty of speech which it affords him as a vantage ground from which he can in safety denounce its works and repudiate its authority. He assumes the right to be in or out of the social system as he chooses. He relies on the general law which protects him, and emancipates himself from some particular law which he finds oppressive to his conscience. He forgets or does not take the trouble to reflect that, if every one were to act as he does, the social machine would come to a stop. He certainly fails to make it clear how a society would subsist in which every man should claim the right of unrestricted disobedience to a law which he happens to think wrong. In fact, it is possible for an over-tender conscience to consort with an insufficient sense of social responsibility. The combination is unfortunate; and we may fairly say that, if the State owes the utmost consideration to the conscience, its owner owes a corresponding debt to the State. With such mutual consideration, and with the development of the civic sense, conflicts between law and conscience are capable of being brought within very narrow limits, though their complete reconciliation will always remain a problem until men are generally agreed as to the fundamental conditions of the social harmony.

It may be asked, on the other hand, whether in insisting on the free development of personality we have not understated the duty of society to its members. We all admit a collective responsibility for children. Are there not grown-up people who stand just as much in need of care? What of the idiot, the imbecile, the feeble-minded or the drunkard? What does rational self-determination mean for these classes? They may injure no one but themselves except by the contagion of bad example. But have we no duty towards them, having in view their own good alone and leaving every other consideration aside? Have we not the right to take the feeble-minded under our care and to keep the drunkard from drink, purely for their own good and apart from every ulterior consideration? And, if so, must we not extend the whole sphere of permissible coercion, and admit that a man may for his own sake and with no ulterior object, be compelled to do what we think right and avoid what we think wrong?

The reply is that the argument is weak just where it seeks to generalize. We are compelled to put the insane under restraint for social reasons apart from their own benefit. But their own benefit would be a fully sufficient reason if no other existed. To them, by their misfortune, liberty, as we understand the term, has no application, because they are incapable of rational choice and therefore of the kind of growth for the sake of which freedom is valuable. The same thing is true of the feeble-minded, and if they are not yet treated on the same principle it is merely because the recognition of their type as a type is relatively modern. But the same thing is also in its degree true of the drunkard, so far as he is the victim of an impulse which he has allowed to grow beyond his own control; and the question whether he should be regarded as a fit object for tutelage or not is to be decided in each case by asking whether such capacity of self-control as he retains would be impaired or repaired by a period of tutelar restraint. There is nothing in all this to touch the essential of liberty which is the value of the power of self-governance where it exists. All that is proved is that where it does not exist it is right to save men from suffering, and if the case admits to put them under conditions in which the normal balance of impulse is most likely to be restored. It may be added that, in the case of the drunkard—and I think the argument applies to all cases where overwhelming impulse is apt to master the will—it is a still more obvious and elementary duty to remove the sources of temptation, and to treat as anti-social in the highest degree every attempt to make profit out of human weakness, misery, and wrong-doing. The case is not unlike that of a very unequal contract. The tempter is coolly seeking his profit, and the sufferer is beset with a fiend within. There is a form of coercion here which the genuine spirit of liberty will not fail to recognize as its enemy, and a form of injury to another which is not the less real because its weapon is an impulse which forces that other to the consent which he yields.

I conclude that there is nothing in the doctrine of liberty to hinder the movement of general will in the sphere in which it is really efficient, and nothing in a just conception of the objects and methods of the general will to curtail liberty in the performance of the functions, social and personal, in which its value lies. Liberty and compulsion have complementary functions, and the self-governing State is at once the product and the condition of the self-governing individual.

Thus there is no difficulty in understanding why the extension of State control on one side goes along with determined resistance to encroachments on another. It is a question not of increasing or diminishing, but of reorganizing, restraints. The period which has witnessed a rapid extension of industrial legislation has seen as determined a resistance to anything like the establishment of doctrinal religious teaching by a State authority,[10] and the distinction is perfectly just. At bottom it is the same conception of liberty and the same conception of the common will that prompts the regulation of industry and the severance of religious worship and doctrinal teaching from the mechanism of State control.

So far we have been considering what the State compels the individual to do. If we pass to the question what the State is to do for the individual, a different but parallel question arises, and we have to note a corresponding movement of opinion. If the State does for the individual what he ought to do for himself what will be the effect on character, initiative, enterprise? It is a question now not of freedom, but of responsibility, and it is one that has caused many searchings of heart, and in respect of which opinion has undergone a remarkable change. Thus, in relation to poverty the older view was that the first thing needful was self-help. It was the business of every man to provide for himself

---

[10] The objection most often taken to "undenominationalism" itself is that it is in reality a form of doctrinal teaching seeking State endowment.

and his family. If, indeed, he utterly failed, neither he nor they could be left to starve, and there was the Poor Law machinery to deal with his case. But the aim of every sincere friend of the poor must be to keep them away from the Poor Law machine. Experience of the forty years before 1834 had taught us what came of free resort to public funds by way of subvention to inadequate wages. It meant simply that the standard of remuneration was lowered in proportion as men could rely on public aid to make good the deficiency, while at the same time the incentives to independent labour were weakened when the pauper stood on an equal footing with the hard-working man. In general, if the attempt was made to substitute for personal effort the help of others, the result would only sap individual initiative and in the end bring down the rate of industrial remuneration. It was thought, for example—and this very point was urged against proposals for Old Age Pensions—that if any of the objects for which a man will, if possible, provide were removed from the scope of his own activity, he would in consequence be content with proportionally lower wages; if the employer was to compensate him for accident, he would fail to make provision for accidents on his own account; if his children were fed by the ratepayers, he would not earn the money wherewith to feed them. Hence, on the one hand, it was urged that the rate of wages would tend to adapt itself to the necessities of the wage earner, that in proportion as his necessities were met from other sources his wages would fall, that accordingly the apparent relief would be in large measure illusory, while finally, in view of the diminished stimulus to individual exertion, the productivity of labour would fall off, the incentives to industry would be diminished, and the community as a whole would be poorer. Upon the other hand, it was conceived that, however deplorable the condition of the working classes might be, the right way of raising them was to trust to individual enterprise and possibly, according to some thinkers, to voluntary combination. By these means the efficiency of labour might be enhanced and its regular remuneration raised. By sternly withholding all external supports we should teach the working classes to stand alone, and if there were pain in the disciplinary process there was yet hope in the future. They would come by degrees to a position of economic independence in which they would be able to face the risks of life, not in reliance upon the State, but by the force of their own brains and the strength of their own right arms.

These views no longer command the same measure of assent. On all sides we find the State making active provision for the poorer classes and not by any means for the destitute alone. We find it educating the children, providing medical inspection, authorizing the feeding of the necessitous at the expense of the ratepayers, helping them to obtain employment through free Labour Exchanges, seeking to organize the labour market with a view to the mitigation of unemployment, and providing old age pensions for all whose incomes fall below thirteen shillings a week, without exacting any contribution. Now, in all this, we may well ask, is the State going forward blindly on the paths of broad and generous but unconsidered charity? Is it and can it remain indifferent to the effect on individual initiative and personal or parental responsibility? Or may we suppose that the wiser heads are well aware of what they are about, have looked at the matter on all sides, and are guided by a reasonable conception of the duty of the State and the responsibilities of the individual? Are we, in fact—for this is really the question—seeking charity or justice?

We said above that it was the function of the State to secure the conditions upon which mind and character may develop themselves. Similarly we may say now that the function of the State is to secure conditions upon which its citizens are able to win by their own efforts all that is necessary to a full civic efficiency. It is not for the State to feed, house, or clothe them. It is for the State to take care that the economic conditions are such that the normal man who is not defective in mind or body or will can by useful labour feed, house, and clothe himself and his family. The "right to work" and the right to a "living wage" are just as valid as the rights of person or property. That is to say, they are integral conditions of a good social order. A society in which a single honest man of normal capacity is definitely unable to find the means of maintaining himself by useful work is to that extent suffering from malorganization. There is somewhere a defect in the social system, a hitch in the economic machine. Now, the individual workman cannot put the machine straight. He is the last person to have any say in the control of the market. It is not his fault if there is over-production in his industry, or if a new and cheaper process has been introduced which makes his particular skill, perhaps the product of years of application, a drug in the market. He does not direct or regulate industry. He is not responsible for its ups and downs, but he has to pay for them. That is why it is not charity but justice for which he is asking. Now, it may be infinitely difficult to meet his demand. To do so may involve a far-reaching economic reconstruction. The industrial questions involved may be so little understood that we may easily make matters worse in the attempt to make them better. All this shows the difficulty in finding means of meeting this particular claim of justice, but it does not shake its position as a claim of justice. A right is a right none the less though the means of securing it be imperfectly known; and the workman who is unemployed or underpaid through economic malorganization will remain a reproach not to the charity but to the justice of society as long as he is to be seen in the land.

If this view of the duty of the State and the right of the workman is coming to prevail, it is owing partly to an enhanced sense of common responsibility, and partly to the teaching of experience. In the earlier days of the Free Trade era, it was permissible to hope that self-help would be an adequate solvent, and that with cheap food and expanding commerce the average workman would be able by the exercise of prudence and thrift not only to maintain himself in good times, but to lay by for sickness, unemployment, and old age. The actual course of events has in large measure disappointed these hopes. It is true that the standard of living in England has progressively advanced throughout the nineteenth century. It is true, in particular, that, since the disastrous period that preceded the Repeal of the Corn Laws and the passing of the Ten Hours' Act, social improvement has been real and marked. Trade Unionism and co-operation have grown, wages upon the whole have increased, the cost of living has diminished, housing and sanitation have improved, the death rate has fallen from about twenty-two to less than fifteen per thousand. But with all this improvement the prospect of a complete and lifelong economic independence for the average workman upon the lines of individual competition, even when supplemented and guarded by the collective bargaining of the Trade Union, appears exceedingly remote. The increase of wages does not appear to be by any means proportionate to the general growth of wealth. The whole standard of living has risen; the very provision of education has brought with it new needs and has almost compelled a higher standard of life in order to satisfy them. As a whole, the working classes of England, though less thrifty than those of some Continental countries, cannot be accused of undue negligence with regard to the future. The accumulation of savings in Friendly Societies, Trade Unions, Co-operative Societies, and Savings Banks shows an increase which has more than kept pace with the rise in the level of wages; yet there appears no likelihood that the average manual worker will attain the goal of that full independence, covering all the risks of life for self and family, which can alone render the competitive system really adequate to the demands of a civilized conscience. The careful researches of Mr. Booth in London and Mr. Rowntree in York, and of others in country districts, have revealed that a considerable percentage of the working classes are actually unable to earn a sum of money representing the full cost of the barest physical necessities for an average family; and, though the bulk of the working classes are undoubtedly in a better position than this, these researches go to show that even the relatively well-to-do gravitate towards this line of primary poverty in seasons of stress, at the time when the children are still at school, for example, or from the moment when the principal wage-earner begins to fail, in the decline of middle life. If only some ten per cent. of the population are actually living upon the poverty line at any given time,[11] twice or three times that number, it is reasonable to suppose, must approach the line in one period or other of their lives. But when we ascend from the conception of a bare physical maintenance for an average family to such a wage as would provide the real minimum requirements of a civilized life and meet all its contingencies without having to lean on any external prop, we should have to make additions to Mr. Rowntree's figure which have not yet been computed, but as to which it is probably well within the mark to say that none but the most highly skilled artisans are able to earn a remuneration meeting the requirements of the case. But, if that is so, it is clear that the system of industrial competition fails to meet the ethical demand embodied in the conception of the "living wage." That system holds out no hope of an improvement which shall bring the means of such a healthy and independent existence as should be the birthright of every citizen of a free state within the grasp of the mass of the people of the

---

[11] I do not include those living in "secondary poverty," as defined by Mr. Rowntree, as the responsibility in this case is partly personal. It must, however, be remembered that great poverty increases the difficulty of efficient management.

United Kingdom. It is this belief slowly penetrating the public mind which has turned it to new thoughts of social regeneration. The sum and substance of the changes that I have mentioned may be expressed in the principle that the individual cannot stand alone, but that between him and the State there is a reciprocal obligation. He owes the State the duty of industriously working for himself and his family. He is not to exploit the labour of his young children, but to submit to the public requirements for their education, health, cleanliness and general well-being. On the other side society owes to him the means of maintaining a civilized standard of life, and this debt is not adequately discharged by leaving him to secure such wages as he can in the higgling of the market.

This view of social obligation lays increased stress on public but by no means ignores private responsibility. It is a simple principle of applied ethics that responsibility should be commensurate with power. Now, given the opportunity of adequately remunerated work, a man has the power to earn his living. It is his right and his duty to make the best use of his opportunity, and if he fails he may fairly suffer the penalty of being treated as a pauper or even, in an extreme case, as a criminal. But the opportunity itself he cannot command with the same freedom. It is only within narrow limits that it comes within the sphere of his control. The opportunities of work and the remuneration for work are determined by a complex mass of social forces which no individual, certainly no individual workman, can shape. They can be controlled, if at all, by the organized action of the community, and therefore, by a just apportionment of responsibility, it is for the community to deal with them.

But this, it will be said, is not Liberalism but Socialism. Pursuing the economic rights of the individual we have been led to contemplate a Socialistic organization of industry. But a word like Socialism has many meanings, and it is possible that there should be a Liberal Socialism, as well as a Socialism that is illiberal. Let us, then, without sticking at a word, seek to follow out the Liberal view of the State in the sphere of economics. Let us try to determine in very general terms what is involved in realizing those primary conditions of industrial well-being which have been laid down, and how they consort with the rights of property and the claims of free industrial enterprise.

CHAPTER VIII

ECONOMIC LIBERALISM

There are two forms of Socialism with which Liberalism has nothing to do. These I will call the mechanical and the official. Mechanical Socialism is founded on a false interpretation of history. It attributes the phenomena of social life and development to the sole operation of the economic factor, whereas the beginning of sound sociology is to conceive society as a whole in which all the parts interact. The economic factor, to take a single point, is at least as much the effect as it is the cause of scientific invention. There would be no world-wide system of telegraphy if there was no need of world-wide intercommunication. But there would be no electric telegraph at all but for the scientific interest which determined the experiments of Gauss and Weber. Mechanical Socialism, further, is founded on a false economic analysis which attributes all value to labour, denying, confounding or distorting the distinct functions of the direction of enterprise, the unavoidable payment for the use of capital, the productivity of nature, and the very complex social forces which, by determining the movements of demand and supply actually fix the rates at which goods exchange with one another. Politically, mechanical Socialism supposes a class war, resting on a clear-cut distinction of classes which does not exist. Far from tending to clear and simple lines of cleavage, modern society exhibits a more and more complex interweaving of interests, and it is impossible for a modern revolutionist to assail "property" in the interest of "labour" without finding that half the "labour" to which he appeals has a direct or indirect interest in "property." As to the future, mechanical Socialism conceives a logically developed system of the control of industry by government. Of this all that need be said is that the construction of Utopias is not a sound method of social science; that this particular Utopia makes insufficient provision for liberty, movement, and growth; and that in order to bring his ideals into the region of practical discussion, what the Socialist needs is to formulate not a system to be substituted as a whole for our present arrangements but a principle to guide statesmanship in the practical work of reforming what is amiss and developing what is good in the actual fabric of industry. A principle so applied grows if it has seeds of good in it, and so in particular the collective control of industry will be extended in proportion as it is found in practice to yield good results. The fancied clearness of Utopian vision is illusory, because its objects are artificial ideas and not living facts. The "system" of the world of books must be reconstructed as a principle that can be applied to the railway, the mine, the workshop, and the office that we know, before it can even be sensibly discussed. The evolution of Socialism as a practical force in politics has, in point of fact, proceeded by such a reconstruction, and this change carries with it the end of the materialistic Utopia.

Official Socialism is a creed of different brand. Beginning with a contempt for ideals of liberty based on a confusion between liberty and competition, it proceeds to a measure of contempt for average humanity in general. It conceives mankind as in the mass a helpless and feeble race, which it is its duty to treat kindly. True kindness, of course, must be combined with firmness, and the life of the average man must be organized for his own good. He need not know that he is being organized. The socialistic organization will work in the background, and there will be wheels within wheels, or rather wires pulling wires. Ostensibly there will be a class of the elect, an aristocracy of character and intellect which will fill the civil services and do the practical work of administration. Behind these will be committees of union and progress who will direct operations, and behind the committees again one or more master minds from whom will emanate the ideas that are to direct the world. The play of democratic government will go on for a time, but the idea of a common will that should actually undertake the organization of social life is held the most childish of illusions. The master minds can for the moment work more easily through democratic forms, because they are here, and to destroy them would cause an upheaval. But the essence of government lies in the method of capture. The ostensible leaders of democracy are ignorant creatures who can with a little management be set to walk in the way in which they should go, and whom the crowd will follow like sheep. The art of governing consists in making men do what you wish without knowing what they are doing, to lead them on without showing them whither until it is too late for them to retrace their steps. Socialism so conceived has in essentials nothing to do with democracy or with liberty. It is a scheme of the organization of life by the superior person, who will decide for each man how he should work, how he should live, and indeed, with the aid of the Eugenist, whether he should live at all or whether he has any business to be born. At any rate, if he ought not to have been born—if, that is, he comes of a stock whose qualities are not approved—the Samurai will take care that he does not perpetuate his race.

Now the average Liberal might have more sympathy with this view of life if he did not feel that for his part he is just a very ordinary man. He is quite sure that he cannot manage the lives of other people for them. He finds it enough to manage his own. But with the leave of the Superior he would rather do this in his own way than in the way of another, whose way may be much wiser but is not his. He would rather marry the woman of his own choice, than the one who would be sure to bring forth children of the standard type. He does not want to be standardized. He does not conceive himself as essentially an item in a census return. He does not want the standard clothes or the standard food, he wants the clothes which he finds comfortable and the food which he likes. With this unregenerate Adam in him, I fear that the Liberalism that is also within him is quite ready to make terms. Indeed, it incites him to go still further. It bids him consider that other men are, on the whole, very like himself and look on life in much the same way, and when it speaks within him of social duty it encourages him to aim not at a position of superiority which will enable him to govern his fellow creatures for their own good, but at a spirit of comradeship in which he will stand shoulder to shoulder with them on behalf of common aims.

If, then, there be such a thing as a Liberal Socialism—and whether there be is still a subject for inquiry—it must clearly fulfil two conditions. In the first place, it must be democratic. It must come from below, not from above. Or rather, it must emerge from the efforts of society as a whole to secure a fuller measure of justice, and a better organization of mutual aid. It must engage the efforts and respond to the genuine desires not of a handful of superior beings, but of great masses of men. And, secondly, and for that very reason, it must make its account with the human individual. It must give the average man free play in the personal life for which he really cares. It must be founded on liberty, and must make not for the suppression but for the development of personality. How far, it may be asked, are these objects compatible? How far is it possible to organize industry in the interest of the common welfare without either overriding the freedom of individual choice or drying up the springs of initiative and energy? How far is it possible to abolish poverty, or to institute economic equality without arresting industrial progress? We cannot put the question without raising more fundamental issues. What is the real meaning of "equality" in economics? Would it mean, for example, that all should enjoy equal rewards, or that equal efforts should enjoy equal rewards, or that equal attainments should enjoy equal rewards? What is the province of justice in economics? Where does justice end and charity begin? And what, behind all this, is the basis of property? What is its social function and value? What is the measure of consideration due to vested interest and prescriptive right? It is impossible, within the limits of a volume, to deal exhaustively with such fundamental questions. The best course will be to follow out the lines of development which appear to proceed from those principles of Liberalism which have been already indicated and to see how far they lead to a solution.

We saw that it was the duty of the State to secure the conditions of self-maintenance for the normal healthy citizen. There are two lines along which the fulfilment of this duty may be sought. One would consist in providing access to the means of production, the other in guaranteeing to the individual a certain share in the common stock. In point of fact, both lines have been followed by Liberal legislation. On the one side this legislation has set itself, however timidly and ineffectively as yet, to reversing the process which divorced the English peasantry from the soil. Contemporary research is making it clear that this divorce was not the inevitable result of slowly operating economic forces. It was brought about by the deliberate policy of the enclosure of the common fields begun in the fifteenth century, partially arrested from the middle of the sixteenth to the eighteenth, and completed between the reigns of George II and Queen Victoria. As this process was furthered by an aristocracy, so there is every reason to hope that it can be successfully reversed by a democracy, and that it will be possible to reconstitute a class of independent peasantry as the backbone of the working population. The experiment, however, involves one form or another of communal ownership. The labourer can only obtain the land with the financial help of the State, and it is certainly not the view of Liberals that the State, having once regained the fee simple, should part with it again. On the contrary, in an equitable division of the fruits of agriculture all advantages that are derived from the qualities or position of the soil itself, or from the enhancement of prices by tariffs would, since they are the product of no man's labour, fall to no man's share, or, what is the same thing, they should fall to every man, that is, to the community. This is why Liberal legislation seeks to create a class not of small landlords but of small tenants. It would give to this class access to the land and would reward them with the fruits of their own work—and no more. The surplus it would take to itself in the form of rent, and while it is desirable to give the State tenant full security against disturbance, rents must at stated periods be adjustable to prices and to cost. So, while Conservative policy is to establish a peasant proprietary which would reinforce the voting strength of property, the Liberal policy is to establish a State tenantry from whose prosperity the whole community would profit. The one solution is individualist. The other, as far as it goes, is nearer to the Socialist ideal.

But, though British agriculture may have a great future before it, it will never regain its dominant position in our economic life, nor are small holdings ever likely to be the prevalent form of agriculture. The bulk of industry is, and probably will be, more and more in the hands of large undertakings with which the individual workman could not compete whatever instruments of production were placed in his hands. For the mass of the people, therefore, to be assured of the means of a decent livelihood must mean to be assured of continuous employment at a living wage, or, as an alternative, of public assistance. Now, as has been remarked, experience goes to show that the wage of the average worker, as fixed by competition, is not and is not likely to become sufficient to cover all the fortunes and misfortunes of life, to provide for sickness, accident, unemployment and old age, in addition to the regular needs of an average family. In the case of accident the State has put the burden of making provision on the employer. In the case of old age it has, acting, as I think, upon a sounder principle, taken the burden upon itself. It is very important to realize precisely what the new departure involved in the Old Age Pensions Act amounted to in point of principle. The Poor Law already guaranteed the aged person and the poor in general against actual starvation. But the Poor Law came into operation only at the point of sheer destitution. It failed to help those who had helped themselves. Indeed, to many it held out little inducement to help themselves if they could not hope to lay by so much as would enable them to live more comfortably on their means than they would live in the workhouse. The pension system throws over the test of destitution. It provides a certain minimum, a basis to go upon, a foundation upon which independent thrift may hope to build up a sufficiency. It is not a narcotic but a stimulus to self help and to friendly aid or filial support, and it is, up to a limit, available for all alike. It is precisely one of the conditions of independence of which voluntary effort can make use, but requiring voluntary effort to make it fully available.

The suggestion underlying the movement for the break up of the Poor Law is just the general application of this principle. It is that, instead of redeeming the destitute, we should seek to render generally available the means of avoiding destitution, though in doing so we should uniformly call on the individual for a corresponding effort on his part. One method of meeting these conditions is to supply a basis for private effort to work upon, as is done in the case of the aged. Another method is that of State-aided insurance, and on these lines Liberal legislators have been experimenting in the hope of dealing with sickness, invalidity, and one portion of the problem of unemployment. A third may be illustrated by the method by which the Minority of the Poor Law Commissioners would deal with the case, at present so often full of tragic import, of the widowed or deserted mother of young children. Hitherto she has been regarded as an object of charity. It has been a matter for the benevolent to help her to retain her home, while it has been regarded as her duty to keep "off the rates" at the cost of no matter what expenditure of labour away from home. The newer conception of rights and duties comes out clearly in the argument of the commissioners, that if we take in earnest all that we say of the duties and responsibilities of motherhood, we shall recognize that the mother of young children is doing better service to the community and one more worthy of pecuniary remuneration when she stays at home and minds her children than when she goes out charing and leaves them to the chances of the street or to the perfunctory care of a neighbour. In proportion as we realize the force of this argument, we reverse our view as to the nature of public assistance in such a case. We no longer consider it desirable to drive the mother out to her charing work if we possibly can, nor do we consider her degraded by receiving public money. We cease, in fact, to regard the public money as a dole, we treat it as a payment for a civic service, and the condition that we are inclined to exact is precisely that she should not endeavour to add to it by earning wages, but rather that she should keep her home respectable and bring up her children in health and happiness.

In defence of the competitive system two arguments have been familiar from old days. One is based on the habits of the working classes. It is said that they spend their surplus incomes on drink, and that if they have no margin for saving, it is because they have sunk it in the public-house. That argument is rapidly being met by the actual change of habits. The wave of temperance which two generations ago reformed the habits of the well-to-do in England is rapidly spreading through all classes in our own time. The drink bill is still excessive, the proportion of his weekly wages spent on drink by the average workman is still too great, but it is a diminishing quantity, and the fear which might have been legitimately expressed in old days that to add to wages was to add to the drink bill could no longer be felt as a valid objection to any improvement in the material condition of the working population in our own time. We no longer find the drink bill heavily increasing in years of commercial prosperity as of old. The second argument has experienced an even more decisive fate. Down to my own time it was forcibly contended that any improvement in the material condition of the mass of the people would result in an increase of the birth rate which, by extending the supply of labour, would bring down wages by an automatic process to the old level. There would be more people and they would all be as miserable as before. The actual decline of the birth rate, whatever its other consequences may be, has driven this argument from the field. The birth rate does not increase with prosperity, but diminishes. There is no fear of over-population; if there is any present danger, it is upon the other side. The fate of these two arguments must be reckoned as a very important factor in the changes of opinion which we have noted.

Nevertheless, it may be thought that the system that I have outlined is no better than a vast organization of State charity, and that as such it must carry the consequences associated with charity on a large scale. It must dry up the sources of energy and undermine the independence of the individual. On the first point, I have already referred to certain cogent arguments for a contrary view. What the State is doing, what it would be doing if the whole series of contemplated changes were carried through to the end, would by no means suffice to meet the needs of the normal man. He would still have to labour to earn his own living. But he would have a basis to go upon, a sub-structure on which it would be possible for him to rear the fabric of a real sufficiency. He would have greater security, a brighter outlook, a more confident hope of being able to keep his head above water. The experience of life suggests that hope is a better stimulus than fear, confidence a better mental environment than insecurity. If desperation will sometimes spur men to exceptional exertion the effect is fleeting, and, for a permanence, a more stable condition is better suited to foster that blend of restraint and energy which makes up the tissue of a life of normal health. There would be those who would abuse their advantages as there are those who abuse every form of social institution. But upon the whole it is thought that individual responsibility can be more clearly fixed and more rigorously insisted on when its legitimate sphere is properly defined, that is to say, when the burden on the shoulders of the individual is not too great for average human nature to bear.

But, it may be urged, any reliance on external assistance is destructive of independence. It is true that to look for support to private philanthropy has this effect, because it makes one man dependent on the good graces of another. But it is submitted that a form of support on which a man can count as a matter of legal right has not necessarily the same effect. Charity, again, tends to diminish the value of independent effort because it flows in the direction of the failures. It is a compensation for misfortune which easily slides into an encouragement to carelessness. What is matter of right, on the other hand, is enjoyed equally by the successful and the unsuccessful. It is not a handicap in favour of the one, but an equal distance deducted from the race to be run against fate by both. This brings us to the real question. Are measures of the kind under discussion to be regarded as measures of philanthropy or measures of justice, as the expression of collective benevolence or as the recognition of a general right? The full discussion of the question involves complex and in some respects novel conceptions of economics and of social ethics to which I can hardly do justice within the limits of this chapter. But I will endeavour to indicate in outline the conception of social and economic justice which underlies the movement of modern Liberal opinion.

We may approach the subject by observing that, whatever the legal theory, in practice the existing English Poor Law recognizes the right of every person to the bare necessaries of life. The destitute man or woman can come to a public authority, and the public authority is bound to give him food and shelter. He has to that extent a lien on the public resources in virtue of his needs as a human being and on no other ground. This lien, however, only operates when he is destitute; and he can only exercise it by submitting to such conditions as the authorities impose, which when the workhouse test is enforced means loss of liberty. It was the leading "principle of 1834" that the lot of the pauper should be made "less eligible" than that of the independent labourer. Perhaps we may express the change of opinion which has come about in our day by saying that according to the newer principle the duty of society is rather to ensure that the lot of the independent labourer be more eligible than that of the pauper. With this object the lien on the common wealth is enlarged and reconstituted. Its exercise does not entail the penal consequence of the loss of freedom unless there is proved misfeasance or neglect on the part of the individual. The underlying contention is that, in a State so wealthy as the United Kingdom, every citizen should have full means of earning by socially useful labour so much material support as experience proves to be the necessary basis of a healthy, civilized existence. And if in the actual working of the industrial system the means are not in actual fact sufficiently available he is held to have a claim not as of charity but as of right on the national resources to make good the deficiency.

That there are rights of property we all admit. Is there not perhaps a general right *to* property? Is there not something radically wrong with an economic system under which through the laws of inheritance and bequest vast inequalities are perpetuated? Ought we to acquiesce in a condition in which the great majority are born to nothing except what they can earn, while some are born to more than the social value of any individual of whatever merit? May it not be that in a reasoned scheme of economic ethics we should have to allow a true right of property in the member of the community as such which would take the form of a certain minimum claim on the public resources? A pretty idea, it may be said, but ethics apart, what are the resources on which the less fortunate is to draw? The British State has little or no collective property available for any such purpose. Its revenues are based on taxation, and in the end what all this means is that the rich are to be taxed for the benefit of the poor, which we may be told is neither justice nor charity but sheer spoliation. To this I would reply that the depletion of public resources is a symptom of profound economic disorganization. Wealth, I would contend, has a social as well as a personal basis. Some forms of wealth, such as ground rents in and about cities, are substantially the creation of society, and it is only through the misfeasance of government in times past that such wealth has been allowed to fall into private hands. Other great sources of wealth are found in financial and speculative operations, often of distinctly anti-social tendency and possible only through the defective organization of our economy. Other causes rest in the partial monopolies which our liquor laws, on the one side, and the old practice of allowing the supply of municipal services to fall into private hands have built up. Through the principle of inheritance, property so accumulated is handed on; and the result is that while there is a small class born to the inheritance of a share in the material benefits of civilization, there is a far larger class which can say "naked we enter, naked we leave." This system, as a whole, it is maintained, requires revision. Property in this condition of things ceases, it is urged, to be essentially an institution by which each man can secure to himself the fruits of his own labour, and becomes an instrument whereby the owner can command the labour of others on terms which he is in general able to dictate. This tendency is held to be undesirable, and to be capable of a remedy through a concerted series of fiscal, industrial, and social measures which would have the effect of augmenting the common stock at the disposal of society, and so applying it as to secure the economic independence of all who do not forfeit their advantages by idleness, incapacity, or crime. There are early forms of communal society in which each person is born to his appropriate status, carrying its appropriate share of the common land. In destroying the last relics of this system economic individualism has laid the basis of great material advances, but at great cost to the happiness of the masses. The ground problem in economics is not to destroy property, but to restore the social conception of property to its right place under conditions suitable to modern needs. This is not to be done by crude measures of redistribution, such as those of which we hear in ancient history. It is to be done by distinguishing the social from the individual factors in wealth, by bringing the elements of social wealth into the public coffers, and by holding it at the disposal of society to administer to the prime needs of its members.

The basis of property is social, and that in two senses. On the one hand, it is the organized force of society that maintains the rights of owners by protecting them against thieves and depredators. In spite of all criticism many people still seem to speak of the rights of property as though they were conferred by Nature or by Providence upon certain fortunate individuals, and as though these individuals had an unlimited right to command the State, as their servant, to secure them by the free use of the machinery of law in the undisturbed enjoyment of their possessions. They forget that without the organized force of society their rights are not worth a week's purchase. They do not ask themselves where they would be without the judge and the policeman and the settled order which society maintains. The prosperous business man who thinks that he has made his fortune entirely by self help does not pause to consider what single step he could have taken on the road to his success but for the ordered tranquillity which has made commercial development possible, the security by road, and rail, and sea, the masses of skilled labour, and the sum of intelligence which civilization has placed at his disposal, the very demand for the goods which he produces which the general progress of the world has created, the inventions which he uses as a matter of course and which have been built up by the collective effort of generations of men of science and organizers of industry. If he dug to the foundations of his fortune he would recognize that, as it is society that maintains and guarantees his possessions, so also it is society which is an indispensable partner in its original creation.

This brings us to the second sense in which property is social. There is a social element in value and a social element in production. In modern industry there is very little that the individual can do by his unaided efforts. Labour is minutely divided; and in proportion as it is divided it is forced to be co-operative. Men produce goods to sell, and the rate of exchange, that is, price, is fixed by relations of demand and supply the rates of which are determined by complex social forces. In the methods of production every man makes use, to the best of his ability, of the whole available means of civilization, of the machinery which the brains of other men have devised, of the human apparatus which is the gift of acquired civilization. Society thus provides conditions or opportunities of which one man will make much better use than another, and the use to which they are put is the individual or personal element in production which is the basis of the personal claim to reward. To maintain and stimulate this personal effort is a necessity of good economic organization, and without asking here whether any particular conception of Socialism would or would not meet this need we may lay down with confidence that no form of Socialism which should ignore it could possibly enjoy enduring success. On the other hand, an individualism which ignores the social factor in wealth will deplete the national resources, deprive the community of its just share in the fruits of industry and so result in a one-sided and inequitable distribution of wealth. Economic justice is to render what is due not only to each individual but to each function, social or personal, that is engaged in the performance of useful service, and this due is measured by the amount necessary to stimulate and maintain the efficient exercise of that useful function. This equation between function and sustenance is the true meaning of economic equality.

Now to apply this principle to the adjustment of the claims of the community on the one hand and the producers or inheritors of wealth on the other would involve a discrimination of the factors of production which is not easy to make in all instances. If we take the case of urban land, referred to above, the distinction is tolerably clear. The value of a site in London is something due essentially to London, not to the landlord. More accurately a part of it is due to London, a part to the British empire, a part, perhaps we should say, to Western civilization. But while it would be impossible to disentangle these subsidiary factors, the main point that the entire increment of value is due to one social factor or another is sufficiently clear, and this explains why Liberal opinion has fastened on the conception of site value as being by right communal and not personal property. The monopoly value of licensed premises, which is the direct creation of laws passed for the control of the liquor traffic, is another case in point. The difficulty which society finds in dealing with these cases is that it has allowed these sources of wealth to pass out of its hands, and that property of these kinds has freely passed from one man to another in the market, in the belief that it stood and would stand on the same basis in law as any other. Hence, it is not possible for society to insist on the whole of its claim. It could only resume its full rights at the cost of great hardship to individuals and a shock to the industrial system. What it can do is to shift taxation step by step from the wealth due to individual enterprise to the wealth that depends on its own collective progress, thus by degrees regaining the ownership of the fruits of its own collective work.

Much more difficult in principle is the question of the more general elements of social value which run through production as a whole. We are dealing here with factors so intricately interwoven in their operation that they can only be separated by an indirect process. What this process would be we may best understand by imagining for a moment a thoroughgoing centralized organization of the industrial system endeavouring to carry out the principles of remuneration outlined above. The central authority which we imagine as endowed with such wisdom and justice as to find for every man his right place and to assign to every man his due reward would, if our argument is sound, find it necessary to assign to each producer, whether working with hand or brain, whether directing a department of industry or serving under direction, such remuneration as would stimulate him to put forth his best efforts and would maintain him in the condition necessary for the life-long exercise of his function. If we are right in considering that a great part of the wealth produced from year to year is of social origin, it would follow that, after the assignment of this remuneration, there would remain a surplus, and this would fall to the coffers of the community and be available for public purposes, for national defence, public works, education, charity, and the furtherance of civilized life.

Now, this is merely an imaginary picture, and I need not ask whether such a measure of wisdom on the part of a Government is practically attainable, or whether such a measure of centralization might not carry consequences which would hamper progress in other directions. The picture serves merely to illustrate the principles of equitable distribution by which the State should be guided in dealing with property. It serves to define our conception of economic justice, and therewith the lines on which we should be guided in the adjustment of taxation and the reorganization of industry. I may illustrate its bearing by taking a couple of cases.

One important source of private wealth under modern conditions is speculation. Is this also a source of social wealth? Does it produce anything for society? Does it perform a function for which our ideal administration would think it necessary to pay? I buy some railway stock at 110. A year or two later I seize a favourable opportunity and sell it at 125. Is the increment earned or unearned? The answer in the single case is clear, but it may be said that my good fortune in this case may be balanced by ill luck in another. No doubt. But, to go no further, if on balance I make a fortune or an income by this method it would seem to be a fortune or an income not earned by productive service. To this it may be replied that the buyers and sellers of stocks are indirectly performing the function of adjusting demand and supply, and so regulating industry. So far as they are expert business men trained in the knowledge of a particular market this may be so. So far as they dabble in the market in the hope of profiting from a favourable turn, they appear rather as gamblers. I will not pretend to determine which of the two is the larger class. I would point out only that, on the face of the facts, the profits derived from this particular source appear to be rather of the nature of a tax which astute or fortunate individuals are able to levy on the producer than as the reward which they obtain for a definite contribution on their own part to production. There are two possible empirical tests of this view. One is that a form of collective organization should be devised which should diminish the importance of the speculative market. Our principle would suggest the propriety of an attempt in that direction whenever opportunity offers. Another would be the imposition of a special tax on incomes derived from this source, and experience would rapidly show whether any such tax would actually hamper the process of production and distribution at any stage. If not, it would justify itself. It would prove that the total profit now absorbed by individuals exceeds, at least by the amount of the tax, the remuneration necessary to maintain that particular economic function.

The other case I will take is that of inherited wealth. This is the main determining factor in the social and economic structure of our time. It is clear on our principle that it stands in quite a different position from that of wealth which is being created from day to day. It can be defended only on two grounds. One is prescriptive right, and the difficulty of disturbing the basis of the economic order. This provides an unanswerable argument against violent and hasty methods, but no argument at all against a gentle and slow-moving policy of economic reorganization. The other argument is that inherited wealth serves several indirect functions. The desire to provide for children and to found a family is a stimulus to effort. The existence of a leisured class affords possibilities for the free development of originality, and a supply of disinterested men and women for the service of the State. I would suggest once again that the only real test to which the value of these arguments can be submitted is the empirical test. On the face of the facts inherited wealth stands on a different footing from acquired wealth, and Liberal policy is on the right lines in beginning the discrimination of earned from unearned income. The distinction is misconceived only so far as income derived from capital or land may represent the savings of the individual and not his inheritance. The true distinction is between the inherited and the acquired, and while the taxation of acquired wealth may operate, so far as it goes, to diminish the profits, and so far to weaken the motive springs, of industry, it is by no means self-evident that any increase of taxation on inherited wealth would necessarily have that effect, or that it would vitally derange any other social function. It is, again, a matter on which only experience can decide, but if experience goes to show that we can impose a given tax on inherited wealth without diminishing the available supply of capital and without losing any service of value, the result would be net gain. The State could never be the sole producer, for in production the personal factor is vital, but there is no limit set by the necessities of things to the extension of its control of natural resources, on the one hand, and the accumulated heritage of the past, on the other.

If Liberal policy has committed itself not only to the discrimination of earned and unearned incomes but also to a super-tax on large incomes from whatever source, the ground principle, again, I take to be a respectful doubt whether any single individual is worth to society by any means as much as some individuals obtain. We might, indeed, have to qualify this doubt if the great fortunes of the world fell to the great geniuses. It would be impossible to determine what we ought to pay for a Shakespere, a Browning, a Newton, or a Cobden. Impossible, but fortunately unnecessary. For the man of genius is forced by his own cravings to give, and the only reward that he asks from society is to be let alone and have some quiet and fresh air. Nor is he in reality entitled, notwithstanding his services, to ask more than the modest sufficiency which enables him to obtain those primary needs of the life of thought and creation, since his creative energy is the response to an inward stimulus which goads him on without regard to the wishes of any one else. The case of the great organizers of industry is rather different, but they, again, so far as their work is socially sound, are driven on more by internal necessity than by the genuine love of gain. They make great profits because their works reach a scale at which, if the balance is on the right side at all, it is certain to be a big balance, and they no doubt tend to be interested in money as the sign of their success, and also as the basis of increased social power. But I believe the direct influence of the lust of gain on this type of mind to have been immensely exaggerated; and as proof I would refer, first, to the readiness of many men of this class to accept and in individual cases actively to promote measures tending to diminish their material gain, and, secondly, to the mass of high business capacity which is at the command of the public administration for salaries which, as their recipient must be perfectly conscious, bear no relation to the income which it would be open to him to earn in commercial competition.

On the whole, then, we may take it that the principle of the super-tax is based on the conception that when we come to an income of some £5,000 a year we approach the limit of the industrial value of the individual.[12] We are not likely to discourage any service of genuine social value by a rapidly increasing surtax on incomes above that amount. It is more likely that we shall quench the anti-social ardour for unmeasured wealth, for social power, and the vanity of display.

These illustrations may suffice to give some concreteness to the conception of economic justice as the maintenance of social function. They serve also to

---

[12] It is true that so long as it remains possible for a certain order of ability to earn £50,000 a year, the community will not obtain its services for £5,000. But if things should be so altered by taxation and economic reorganization that £5,000 became in practice the highest limit attainable, and remained attainable even for the ablest only by effort, there is no reason to doubt that that effort would be forthcoming. It is not the absolute amount of remuneration, but the increment of remuneration in proportion to the output of industrial or commercial capacity, which serves as the needed stimulus to energy.

show that the true resources of the State are larger and more varied than is generally supposed. The true function of taxation is to secure to society the element in wealth that is of social origin, or, more broadly, all that does not owe its origin to the efforts of living individuals. When taxation, based on these principles, is utilized to secure healthy conditions of existence to the mass of the people it is clear that this is no case of robbing Peter to pay Paul. Peter is not robbed. Apart from the tax it is he who would be robbing the State. A tax which enables the State to secure a certain share of social value is not something deducted from that which the taxpayer has an unlimited right to call his own, but rather a repayment of something which was all along due to society.

But why should the proceeds of the tax go to the poor in particular? Granting that Peter is not robbed, why should Paul be paid? Why should not the proceeds be expended on something of common concern to Peter and Paul alike, for Peter is equally a member of the community? Undoubtedly the only just method of dealing with the common funds is to expend them in objects which subserve the common good, and there are many directions in which public expenditure does in fact benefit all classes alike. This, it is worth noting, is true even of some important branches of expenditure which in their direct aim concern the poorer classes. Consider, for example, the value of public sanitation, not merely to the poorer regions which would suffer first if it were withheld, but to the richer as well who, seclude themselves as they may, cannot escape infection. In the old days judge and jury, as well as prisoners, would die of gaol fever. Consider, again, the economic value of education, not only to the worker, but to the employer whom he will serve. But when all this is allowed for it must be admitted that we have throughout contemplated a considerable measure of public expenditure in the elimination of poverty. The prime justification of this expenditure is that the prevention of suffering from the actual lack of adequate physical comforts is an essential element in the common good, an object in which all are bound to concern themselves, which all have the right to demand and the duty to fulfil. Any common life based on the avoidable suffering even of one of those who partake in it is a life not of harmony, but of discord.

But we can go further. We said at the outset that the function of society was to secure to all normal adult members the means of earning by useful work the material necessaries of a healthy and efficient life. We can see now that this is one case and, properly understood, the largest and most far reaching case falling under the general principle of economic justice. This principle lays down that every social function must receive the reward that is sufficient to stimulate and maintain it through the life of the individual. Now, how much this reward may be in any case it is probably impossible to determine otherwise than by specific experiment. But if we grant, in accordance with the idea with which we have been working all along, that it is demanded of all sane adult men and women that they should live as civilized beings, as industrious workers, as good parents, as orderly and efficient citizens, it is, on the other side, the function of the economic organization of society to secure them the material means of living such a life, and the immediate duty of society is to mark the points at which such means fail and to make good the deficiency. Thus the conditions of social efficiency mark the minimum of industrial remuneration, and if they are not secured without the deliberate action of the State they must be secured by means of the deliberate action of the State. If it is the business of good economic organization to secure the equation between function and maintenance, the first and greatest application of this principle is to the primary needs. These fix the minimum standard of remuneration beyond which we require detailed experiment to tell us at what rate increased value of service rendered necessitates corresponding increase of reward.

It may be objected that such a standard is unattainable. There are those, it may be contended, who are not, and never will be, worth a full efficiency wage. Whatever is done to secure them such a remuneration will only involve net loss. Hence it violates our standard of economic justice. It involves payment for a function of more than it is actually worth, and the discrepancy might be so great as to cripple society. It must, of course, be admitted that the population contains a certain percentage of the physically incapable, the mentally defective, and the morally uncontrolled. The treatment of these classes, all must agree, is and must be based on other principles than those of economics. One class requires punitive discipline, another needs life-long care, a third—the mentally and morally sound but physically defective—must depend, to its misfortune, on private and public charity. There is no question here of payment for a function, but of ministering to human suffering. It is, of course, desirable on economic as well as on broader grounds that the ministration should be so conceived as to render its object as nearly as possible independent and self-supporting. But in the main all that is done for these classes of the population is, and must be, a charge on the surplus. The real question that may be raised by a critic is whether the considerable proportion of the working class whose earnings actually fall short, as we should contend, of the minimum, could in point of fact earn that minimum. Their actual value, he may urge, is measured by the wage which they do in fact command in the competitive market, and if their wage falls short of the standard society may make good the deficiency if it will and can, but must not shut its eyes to the fact that in doing so it is performing, not an act of economic justice, but of charity. To this the reply is that the price which naked labour without property can command in bargaining with employers who possess property is no measure at all of the addition which such labour can actually make to wealth. The bargain is unequal, and low remuneration is itself a cause of low efficiency which in turn tends to react unfavourably on remuneration. Conversely, a general improvement in the conditions of life reacts favourably on the productivity of labour. Real wages have risen considerably in the last half century, but the income-tax returns indicate that the wealth of the business and professional man has increased even more rapidly. Up to the efficiency minimum there is, then, every reason to think that a general increase of wages would positively increase the available surplus whether that surplus goes to individuals as profits or to the State as national revenue. The material improvement of working-class conditions will more than pay its way regarded purely as an economic investment on behalf of society.

This conclusion is strengthened if we consider narrowly what elements of cost the "living wage" ought in principle to cover. We are apt to assume uncritically that the wages earned by the labour of an adult man ought to suffice for the maintenance of an average family, providing for all risks. It ought, we think, to cover not only the food and clothing of wife and children, but the risks of sickness, accident, and unemployment. It ought to provide for education and lay by for old age. If it fails we are apt to think that the wage earner is not self supporting. Now, it is certainly open to doubt whether the actual addition to wealth made by an unskilled labourer denuded of all inherited property would equal the cost represented by the sum of these items. But here our further principle comes into play. He ought not to be denuded of all inherited property. As a citizen he should have a certain share in the social inheritance. This share should be his support in the times of misfortune, of sickness, and of worklessness, whether due to economic disorganization or to invalidity and old age. His children's share, again, is the State-provided education. These shares are charges on the social surplus. It does not, if fiscal arrangements are what they should be, infringe upon the income of other individuals, and the man who without further aid than the universally available share in the social inheritance which is to fall to him as a citizen pays his way through life is to be justly regarded as self-supporting.

The central point of Liberal economics, then, is the equation of social service and reward. This is the principle that every function of social value requires such remuneration as serves to stimulate and maintain its effective performance; that every one who performs such a function has the right, in the strict ethical sense of that term, to such remuneration and to no more; that the residue of existing wealth should be at the disposal of the community for social purposes. Further, it is the right, in the same sense, of every person capable of performing some useful social function that he should have the opportunity of so doing, and it is his right that the remuneration that he receives for it should be his property, i. e. that it should stand at his free disposal enabling him to direct his personal concerns according to his own preferences. These are rights in the sense that they are conditions of the welfare of its members which a well-ordered State will seek by every means to fulfil. But it is not suggested that the way of such fulfilment is plain, or that it could be achieved at a stroke by a revolutionary change in the tenure of property or the system of industry. It is, indeed, implied that the State is vested with a certain overlordship over property in general and a supervisory power over industry in general, and this principle of economic sovereignty may be set side by side with that of economic justice as a no less fundamental conception of economic Liberalism. For here, as elsewhere, liberty implies control. But the manner in which the State is to exercise its controlling power is to be learnt by experience and even in large measure by cautious experiment. We have sought to determine the principle which should guide its action, the ends at which it is to aim. The systematic study of the means lies rather within the province of economics; and the teaching of history seems to be that progress is more continuous and secure when men are content to deal with problems piecemeal than when they seek to destroy root and branch in order to erect a complete system which has captured the imagination.

It is evident that these conceptions embody many of the ideas that go to make up the framework of Socialist teaching, though they also emphasize elements of individual right and personal independence, of which Socialism at times appears oblivious. The distinction that I would claim for economic Liberalism is that it seeks to do justice to the social and individual factors in industry alike, as opposed to an abstract Socialism which emphasizes the one side and an abstract Individualism which leans its whole weight on the other. By keeping to the conception of harmony as our clue we constantly define the rights of the individual in terms of the common good, and think of the common good in terms of the welfare of all the individuals who constitute a society. Thus in economics we avoid the confusion of liberty with competition, and see no virtue in the right of a man to get the better of others. At the same time we are not led to minimize the share of personal initiative, talent, or energy in production, but are free to contend for their claim to adequate recognition. A Socialist who is convinced of the logical coherence and practical applicability of his system may dismiss such endeavours to harmonize divergent claims as a half-hearted and illogical series of compromises. It is equally possible that a Socialist who conceives Socialism as consisting in essence in the co-operative organization of industry by consumers, and is convinced that the full solution of industrial problems lies in that direction, should in proportion as he considers the psychological factors in production and investigates the means of realizing his ideal, find himself working back along the path to a point where he will meet the men who are grappling with the problems of the day on the principles here suggested, and will find himself able to move forward in practice in the front ranks of economic Liberalism. If this is so, the growing co-operation of political Liberalism and Labour, which in the last few years has replaced the antagonism of the 'nineties, is no mere accident of temporary political convenience, but has its roots deep in the necessities of Democracy.

CHAPTER IX

THE FUTURE OF LIBERALISM

The nineteenth century might be called the age of Liberalism, yet its close saw the fortunes of that great movement brought to their lowest ebb. Whether at home or abroad those who represented Liberal ideas had suffered crushing defeats. But this was the least considerable of the causes for anxiety. If Liberals had been defeated, something much worse seemed about to befall Liberalism. Its faith in itself was waxing cold. It seemed to have done its work. It had the air of a creed that is becoming fossilized as an extinct form, a fossil that occupied, moreover, an awkward position between two very active and energetically moving grindstones—the upper grindstone of plutocratic imperialism, and the nether grindstone of social democracy. "We know all about you," these parties seemed to say to Liberalism; "we have been right through you and come out on the other side. Respectable platitudes, you go maundering on about Cobden and Gladstone, and the liberty of the individual, and the rights of nationality, and government by the people. What you say is not precisely untrue, but it is unreal and uninteresting." So far in chorus. "It is not up to date," finished the Imperialist, and the Socialist bureaucrat. "It is not bread and butter," finished the Social democrat. Opposed in everything else, these two parties agreed in one thing. They were to divide the future between them. Unfortunately, however, for their agreement, the division was soon seen to be no equal one. Whatever might be the ultimate recuperative power of Social Democracy, for the time being, in the paralysis of Liberalism, the Imperial reaction had things all to itself. The governing classes of England were to assert themselves. They were to consolidate the Empire, incidentally passing the steam roller over two obstructive republics. They were to "teach the law" to the "sullen new-caught peoples" abroad. They were to re-establish the Church at home by the endowment of doctrinal education. At the same time they were to establish the liquor interest—which is, after all, the really potent instrument of government from above. They were to bind the colonies to us by ties of fiscal preference, and to establish the great commercial interests on the basis of protection. Their government, as conceived by the best exponents of the new doctrine, was by no means to be indifferent to the humanitarian claims of the social conscience. They were to deal out factory acts, and establish wages boards. They were to make an efficient and a disciplined people. In the idea of discipline the military element rapidly assumed a greater prominence. But on this side the evolution of opinion passed through two well-marked phases. The first was the period of optimism and expansion. The Englishman was the born ruler of the world. He might hold out a hand of friendship to the German and the American, whom he recognized as his kindred and who lived within the law. The rest of the world was peopled by dying nations whose manifest destiny was to be "administered" by the coming races, and exploited by their commercial syndicates. This mood of optimism did not survive the South African War. It received its death-blow at

Colenso and Magersfontein, and within a few years fear had definitely taken the place of ambition as the mainspring of the movement to national and imperial consolidation. The Tariff Reform movement was largely inspired by a sense of insecurity in our commercial position. The half-patronizing friendship for Germany rapidly gave way, first to commercial jealousy, and then to unconcealed alarm for our national safety. All the powers of society were bent on lavish naval expenditure, and of imposing the idea of compulsory service on a reluctant people. The disciplined nation was needed no longer to dominate the world, but to maintain its own territory.

Now, we are not concerned here to follow up the devious windings of modern Conservatism. We have to note only that what modern democracy has to face is no mere inertia of tradition. It is a distinct reactionary policy with a definite and not incoherent creed of its own, an ideal which in its best expression—for example, in the daily comments of the *Morning Post*—is certain to exercise a powerful attraction on many generous minds—the ideal of the efficient, disciplined nation, centre and dominating force of a powerful, self-contained, militant empire. What concerns us more particularly is the reaction of Conservative development upon the fortunes of democracy. But to understand this reaction, and, indeed, to make any sound estimate of the present position and prospects of Liberalism, we must cast a rapid glance over the movement of progressive thought during the last generation. When Gladstone formed his second Government in 1880 the old party system stood secure in Great Britain. It was only a band of politicians from the other side of St. George's Channel who disowned both the great allegiances. For the British political mind the plain distinction of Liberal and Conservative held the field, and the division was not yet a class distinction. The great Whig families held their place, and they of the aristocratic houses divided the spoil. But a new leaven was at work. The prosperity which had culminated in 1872 was passing away. Industrial progress slowed down; and, though the advance from the "Hungry 'Forties" had been immense, men began to see the limit of what they could reasonably expect from retrenchment and Free Trade. The work of Mr. Henry George awakened new interest in problems of poverty, and the idealism of William Morris gave new inspiration to Socialist propaganda. Meanwhile, the teaching of Green and the enthusiasm of Toynbee were setting Liberalism free from the shackles of an individualist conception of liberty and paving the way for the legislation of our own time. Lastly, the Fabian Society brought Socialism down from heaven and established a contact with practical politics and municipal government. Had Great Britain been an island in the mid-Pacific the onward movement would have been rapid and undeviating in its course. As it was, the new ideas were reflected in the parliament and the cabinet of 1880-1885, and the Radicalism of Birmingham barely kept on terms with the Whiggery of the clubs. A redistribution of social forces which would amalgamate the interests of "property" on the one side and those of democracy on the other was imminent, and on social questions democracy reinforced by the enfranchisement of the rural labourers in 1884 stood to win. At this stage the Irish question came to a head. Mr. Gladstone declared for Home Rule, and the party fissure took place on false lines. The upper and middle classes in the main went over to Unionism, but they took with them a section of the Radicals, while Mr. Gladstone's personal force retained on the Liberal side a number of men whose insight into the needs of democracy was by no means profound. The political fight was for the moment shifted from the social question to the single absorbing issue of Home Rule, and the new Unionist party enjoyed twenty years of almost unbroken supremacy. Again, had the Home Rule issue stood alone it might have been settled in 1892, but meanwhile in the later 'eighties the social question had become insistent. Socialism, ceasing to be a merely academic force, had begun to influence organized labour, and had inspired the more generous minds among the artisans with the determination to grapple with the problem of the unskilled workmen. From the Dockers' strike of 1889 the New Unionism became a fighting force in public affairs, and the idea of a Labour party began to take shape. On the new problems Liberalism, weakened as it already had been, was further divided, and its failure in 1892 is to be ascribed far more to this larger cause than to the dramatic personal incident of the Parnell divorce. In office without legislative power from 1892 to 1895, the Liberal party only experienced further loss of credit, and the rise of Imperialism swept the whole current of public interest in a new direction. The Labour movement itself was paralyzed, and the defeat of the Engineers in 1897 put an end to the hope of achieving a great social transformation by the method of the strike. But, in the meanwhile, opinion was being silently transformed. The labours of Mr. Charles Booth and his associates had at length stated the problem of poverty in scientific terms. Social and economic history was gradually taking shape as a virtually new branch of knowledge. The work of Mr. and Mrs. Sidney Webb helped to clear up the relations between the organized efforts of workmen and the functions of the State. The discerning observer could trace the "organic filaments" of a fuller and more concrete social theory.

On the other hand, in the Liberal ranks many of the most influential men had passed, without consciousness of the transition, under the sway of quite opposite influences. They were becoming Imperialists in their sleep, and it was only as the implications of Imperialism became evident that they were awakened. It was with the outbreak of the South African War that the new development of Conservative policy first compelled the average Liberal to consider his position. It needed the shock of an outspoken violation of right to stir him; and we may date the revival of the idea of justice in the party as an organized force from the speech in the summer of 1901 in which Sir Henry Campbell-Bannerman set himself against the stream of militant sentiment and challenged in a classic phrase the methods of the war. From the day of this speech, which was supposed at the time to have irretrievably ruined his political career, the name of the party-leader, hitherto greeted with indifference, became a recognized signal for the cheers of a political meeting, and a man with no marked genius but that of character and the insight which character gave into the minds of his followers acquired in his party the position of a Gladstone. This was the first and fundamental victory, the reinstatement of the idea of Right in the mind of Liberalism. Then, as the Conservative attack developed and its implications became apparent, one interest after another of the older Liberalism was rudely shaken into life. The Education Act of 1902 brought the Nonconformists into action. The Tariff Reform movement put Free Trade on its defence, and taught men to realize what the older economics of Liberalism had done for them. The Socialists of practical politics, the Labour Party, found that they could by no means dispense with the discipline of Cobden. Free Trade finance was to be the basis of social reform. Liberalism and Labour learned to co-operate in resisting delusive promises of remedies for unemployment and in maintaining the right of free international exchange. Meanwhile, Labour itself had experienced the full brunt of the attack. It had come not from the politicians but from the judges, but in this country we have to realize that within wide limits the judges are in effect legislators, and legislators with a certain persistent bent which can be held in check only by the constant vigilance and repeated efforts of the recognized organ for the making and repeal of law. In destroying the old position of the Trade Unions, the judges created the modern Labour party and cemented its alliance with Liberalism. Meanwhile, the aftermath of Imperialism in South Africa was reaped, and Conservative disillusionment unlocked the floodgates for the advancing tide of the Liberal revival.

The tide has by no means spent itself. If it no longer rushes in an electoral torrent as in 1906 it flows in a steady stream towards social amelioration and democratic government. In this movement it is now sufficiently clear to all parties that the distinctive ideas of Liberalism have a permanent function. The Socialist recognizes with perfect clearness, for example, that popular government is not a meaningless shibboleth, but a reality that has to be maintained and extended by fighting. He is well aware that he must deal with the House of Lords and the Plural vote if he is to gain his own ends. He can no longer regard these questions as difficulties interposed by half-hearted Liberals to distract attention from the Social problem. He is aware that the problem of Home Rule and of devolution generally is an integral part of the organization of democracy. And, as a rule, he not merely acquiesces in the demand of women for a purely political right, but only quarrels with the Liberal party for its tardiness in meeting the demand. The old Liberal idea of peace and retrenchment again is recognized by the Socialistic, and indeed by the whole body of social reformers, as equally essential for the successful prosecution of their aims. Popular budgets will bring no relief to human suffering if the revenues that they secure are all to go upon the most expensive ship that is the fashion of the moment, nor can the popular mind devote itself to the improvement of domestic conditions while it is distracted either by ambitions or by scares. On the other side, the Liberal who starts from the Gladstonian tradition has in large measure realized that if he is to maintain the essence of his old ideas it must be through a process of adaptation and growth. He has learnt that while Free Trade laid the foundations of prosperity it did not erect the building. He has to acknowledge that it has not solved the problems of unemployment, of underpayment, of overcrowding. He has to look deeper into the meaning of liberty and to take account of the bearing of actual conditions on the meaning of equality. As an apostle of peace and an opponent of swollen armaments, he has come to recognize that the expenditure of the social surplus upon the instruments of progress is the real alternative to its expenditure on the instruments of war. As a Temperance man he is coming to rely more on the indirect effect of social improvement on the one hand and the elimination of monopolist profit on the other, than on the uncertain chances of absolute prohibition.

There are, then, among the composite forces which maintained the Liberal Government in power through the crisis of 1910, the elements of such an organic view as may inspire and direct a genuine social progress. Liberalism has passed through its Slough of Despond, and in the give and take of ideas with Socialism has learnt, and taught, more than one lesson. The result is a broader and deeper movement in which the cooler and clearer minds recognize below the differences of party names and in spite of certain real cross-currents a genuine unity of purpose. What are the prospects of this movement? Will it be maintained? Is it the steady stream to which we have compared it, or a wave which must gradually sink into the trough?

To put this question is to ask in effect whether democracy is in substance as well as in form a possible mode of government. To answer this question we must ask what democracy really means, and why it is the necessary basis of the Liberal idea. The question has already been raised incidentally, and we have seen reason to dismiss both the individualist and the Benthamite argument for popular government as unsatisfactory. We even admitted a doubt whether some of the concrete essentials of liberty and social justice might not, under certain conditions, be less fully realized under a widely-extended suffrage than under the rule of a superior class or a well-ordered despotism. On what, then, it may be asked, do we found our conception of democracy? Is it on general principles of social philosophy, or on the special conditions of our own country or of contemporary civilization? And how does our conception relate itself to our other ideas of the social order? Do we assume that the democracy will in the main accept these ideas, or if it rejects them are we willing to acquiesce in its decision as final? And in the end what do we expect? Will democracy assert itself, will it find a common purpose and give it concrete shape? Or will it blunder on, the passive subject of scares and ambitions, frenzies of enthusiasm and dejection, clay in the hands of those whose profession it is to model it to their will.

First as to the general principle. Democracy is not founded merely on the right or the private interest of the individual. This is only one side of the shield. It is founded equally on the function of the individual as a member of the community. It founds the common good upon the common will, in forming which it bids every grown-up, intelligent person to take a part. No doubt many good things may be achieved for a people without responsive effort on its own part. It may be endowed with a good police, with an equitable system of private law, with education, with personal freedom, with a well-organized industry. It may receive these blessings at the hands of a foreign ruler, or from an enlightened bureaucracy or a benevolent monarch. However obtained, they are all very good things. But the democratic theory is that, so obtained, they lack a vitalizing element. A people so governed resembles an individual who has received all the external gifts of fortune, good teachers, healthy surroundings, a fair breeze to fill his sails, but owes his prosperous voyage to little or no effort of his own. We do not rate such a man so high as one who struggles through adversity to a much less eminent position. What we possess has its intrinsic value, but how we came to possess it is also an important question. It is so with a society. Good government is much, but the good will is more, and even the imperfect, halting, confused utterance of the common will may have in it the potency of higher things than a perfection of machinery can ever attain.

But this principle makes one very large assumption. It postulates the existence of a common will. It assumes that the individuals whom it would enfranchise can enter into the common life and contribute to the formation of a common decision by a genuine interest in public transactions. Where and in so far as this assumption definitely fails, there is no case for democracy. Progress, in such a case, is not wholly impossible, but it must depend on the number of those who do care for the things that are of social value, who advance knowledge or "civilize life through the discoveries of art," or form a narrow but effective public opinion in support of liberty and order. We may go further. Whatever the form of government progress always does in fact depend on those who so think and live, and on the degree in which these common interests envelop their life and thought. Now, complete and wholehearted absorption in public interests is rare. It is the property not of the mass but of the few, and the democrat is well aware that it is the remnant which saves the people. He subjoins only that if their effort is really to succeed the people must be willing to be saved. The masses who spend their toilsome days in mine or factory struggling for bread have not their heads for ever filled with the complex details of international policy or industrial law. To expect this would be absurd. What is not exaggerated is to expect them to respond and assent to the things that make for the moral and material welfare of the country, and the position of the democrat is that the "remnant" is better occupied in convincing the people and carrying their minds and wills with it than in imposing on them laws which they are concerned only to obey and enjoy. At the same time, the remnant, be it never so select, has always much to learn. Some men are much better and wiser than others, but experience seems to show that hardly any man is so much better or wiser than others that he can permanently stand the test of irresponsible power over them. On the contrary, the best and wisest is he who is ready to go to the humblest in a spirit of inquiry, to find out what he wants and why he wants it before seeking to legislate for him. Admitting the utmost that can be said for the necessity of leadership, we must at the same time grant that the perfection of leadership itself lies in securing the willing, convinced, open-eyed support of the mass.

Thus individuals will contribute to the social will in very varying degrees, but the democratic thesis is that the formation of such a will, that is, in effect, the extension of intelligent interest in all manner of public things, is in itself a good, and more than that, it is a condition qualifying other good things. Now the extension of interest is not to be created by democratic forms of government, and if it neither exists nor can be brought into existence, democracy remains an empty form and may even be worse than useless. On the other hand, where the capacity exists the establishment of responsible government is the first condition of its development. Even so it is not the sole condition. The modern State is a vast and complex organism. The individual voter feels himself lost among the millions. He is imperfectly acquainted with the devious issues and large problems of the day, and is sensible how little his solitary vote can affect their decision. What he needs to give him support and direction is organization with his neighbours and fellow workers. He can understand, for example, the affairs of his trade union, or, again, of his chapel. They are near to him. They affect him, and he feels that he can affect them. Through these interests, again, he comes into touch with wider questions—with a Factory Bill or an Education Bill—and in dealing with these questions he will now act as one of an organized body, whose combined voting strength will be no negligible quantity. Responsibility comes home to him, and to bring home responsibility is the problem of all government. The development of social interest—and that is democracy—depends not only on adult suffrage and the supremacy of the elected legislature, but on all the intermediate organizations which link the individual to the whole. This is one among the reasons why devolution and the revival of local government, at present crushed in this country by a centralized bureaucracy, are of the essence of democratic progress.

The success of democracy depends on the response of the voters to the opportunities given them. But, conversely, the opportunities must be given in order to call forth the response. The exercise of popular government is itself an education. In considering whether any class or sex or race should be brought into the circle of enfranchisement, the determining consideration is the response which that class or sex or race would be likely to make to the trust. Would it enter effectively into the questions of public life, or would it be so much passive voting material, wax in the hands of the less scrupulous politicians? The question is a fair one, but people are too ready to answer it in the less favourable sense on the ground of the actual indifference or ignorance which they find or think they find among the unenfranchised. They forget that in that regard enfranchisement itself may be precisely the stimulus needed to awaken interest, and while they are impressed with the danger of admitting ignorant and irresponsible, and perhaps corruptible voters to a voice in the government, they are apt to overlook the counterbalancing danger of leaving a section of the community outside the circle of civic responsibility. The actual work of government must affect, and also it must be affected by, its relation to all who live within the realm. To secure good adaptation it ought, I will not say to reflect, but at least to take account of, the dispositions and circumstances of every class in the population. If any one class is dumb, the result is that Government is to that extent uninformed. It is not merely that the interests of that class may suffer, but that, even with the best will, mistakes may be made in handling it, because it cannot speak for itself. Officious spokesmen will pretend to represent its views, and will obtain, perhaps, undue authority merely because there is no way of bringing them to book. So among ourselves does the press constantly represent public opinion to be one thing while the cold arithmetic of the polls conclusively declares it to be another. The ballot alone effectively liberates the quiet citizen from the tyranny of the shouter and the wire-puller.

I conclude that an impression of existing inertness or ignorance is not a sufficient reason for withholding responsible government or restricting the area of the suffrage. There must be a well-grounded view that political incapacity is so deep-rooted that the extension of political rights would tend only to facilitate undue influence by the less scrupulous sections of the more capable part of the people. Thus where we have an oligarchy of white planters in the midst of a coloured population, it is always open to doubt whether a general colour-franchise will be a sound method of securing even-handed justice. The economic and social conditions may be such that the "coloured" man would just have to vote as his master told him, and if the elementary rights are to be secured for all it may be that a semi-despotic system like that of some of our Crown colonies is the best that can be devised. On the other side, that which is most apt to frighten a governing class or race, a clamour on the part of an unenfranchised people for political rights, is to the democrat precisely the strongest reason that he can have in the absence of direct experience for believing them fit for the exercise of civic responsibility. He welcomes signs of dissatisfaction among the disfranchised as the best proof of awakening interest in public affairs, and he has none of those fears of ultimate social disruption which are a nightmare to bureaucracies because experience has sufficiently proved to him the healing power of freedom, of responsibility, and of the sense of justice. Moreover, a democrat cannot be a democrat for his own country alone. He cannot but recognize the complex and subtle interactions of nation upon nation which make every local success or failure of democracy tell upon other countries. Nothing has been more encouraging to the Liberalism of Western Europe in recent years than the signs of political awakening in the East. Until yesterday it seemed as though it would in the end be impossible to resist the ultimate "destiny" of the white races to be masters of the rest of the world. The result would have been that, however far democracy might develop within any Western State, it would always be confronted with a contrary principle in the relation of that State to dependencies, and this contradiction, as may easily be seen by the attentive student of our own political constitutions, is a standing menace to domestic freedom. The awakening of the Orient, from Constantinople to Pekin, is the greatest and most hopeful political fact of our time, and it is with the deepest shame that English Liberals have been compelled to look on while our Foreign Office has made itself the accomplice in the attempt to nip Persian freedom in the bud, and that in the interest of the most ruthless tyranny that has ever crushed the liberties of a white people.

The cause of democracy is bound up with that of internationalism. The relation is many-sided. It is national pride, resentment, or ambition one day that sweeps the public mind and diverts it from all interest in domestic progress. The next day the same function is performed no less adequately by a scare. The practice of playing on popular emotions has been reduced to a fine art which neither of the great parties is ashamed to employ. Military ideals possess the mind, and military expenditure eats up the public resources. On the other side, the political economic and social progress of other nations reacts on our own. The backwardness of our commercial rivals in industrial legislation was long made an argument against further advances among ourselves. Conversely, when they go beyond us, as now they often do, we can learn from them. Physically the world is rapidly becoming one, and its unity must ultimately be reflected in political institutions. The old doctrine of absolute sovereignty is dead. The greater States of the day exhibit a complex system of government within government, authority limited by authority, and the world-state of the not impossible future must be based on a free national self-direction as full and satisfying as that enjoyed by Canada or Australia within the British Empire at this moment. National emulation will express itself less in the desire to extend territory or to count up ships and guns, and more in the endeavour to magnify the contribution of our own country to civilized life. Just as in the rebirth of our municipal life we find a civic patriotism which takes interest in the local university, which feels pride in the magnitude of the local industry, which parades the lowest death rate in the country, which is honestly ashamed of a bad record for crime or pauperism, so as Englishmen we shall concern ourselves less with the question whether two of our Dreadnoughts might not be pitted against one German, and more with the question whether we cannot equal Germany in the development of science, of education, and of industrial technique. Perhaps even, recovering from our present artificially induced and radically insincere mood of national self-abasement, we shall learn to take some pride in our own characteristic contributions as a nation to the arts of government, to the thought, the literature, the art, the mechanical inventions which have made and are re-making modern civilization.

Standing by national autonomy and international equality, Liberalism is necessarily in conflict with the Imperial idea as it is ordinarily presented. But this is not to say that it is indifferent to the interests of the Empire as a whole, to the sentiment of unity pervading its white population, to all the possibilities involved in the bare fact that a fourth part of the human race recognizes one flag and one supreme authority. In relation to the self-governing colonies the Liberal of today has to face a change in the situation since Cobden's time not unlike that which we have traced in other departments. The Colonial Empire as it stands is in substance the creation of the older Liberalism. It is founded on self-government, and self-government is the root from which the existing sentiment of unity has sprung. The problem of our time is to devise means for the more concrete and living expression of this sentiment without impairing the rights of self-government on which it depends. Hitherto the "Imperialist" has had matters all his own way and has cleverly exploited Colonial opinion, or an appearance of Colonial opinion, in favour of class ascendancy and reactionary legislation in the mother country. But the colonies include the most democratic communities in the world. Their natural sympathies are not with the Conservatives, but with the most Progressive parties in the United Kingdom. They favour Home Rule, they set the pace in social legislation. There exist accordingly the political conditions of a democratic alliance which it is the business of the British Liberal to turn to account. He may hope to make his country the centre of a group of self-governing, democratic communities, one of which, moreover, serves as a natural link with the other great commonwealth of English-speaking people. The constitutional mechanism of the new unity begins to take shape in the Imperial Council, and its work begins to define itself as the adjustment of interests as between different portions of the Empire and the organization of common defence. Such a union is no menace to the world's peace or to the cause of freedom. On the contrary, as a natural outgrowth of a common sentiment, it is one of the steps towards a wider unity which involves no backstroke against the ideal of self-government. It is a model, and that on no mean scale, of the International State.

Internationalism on the one side, national self-government on the other, are the radical conditions of the growth of a social mind which is the essence, as opposed to the form, of democracy. But as to form itself a word must, in conclusion, be said. If the forms are unsuitable the will cannot express itself, and if it fails of adequate expression it is in the end thwarted, repressed and paralyzed. In the matter of form the inherent difficulty of democratic government, whether direct or representative, is that it is government by majority, not government by universal consent. Its decisions are those of the larger part of the people, not of the whole. This defect is an unavoidable consequence of the necessities of decision and the impossibility of securing universal agreement. Statesmen have sought to remedy it by applying something of the nature of a brake upon the process of change. They have felt that to justify a new departure of any magnitude there must be something more than a bare majority. There must either be a large majority, two-thirds or three-fourths of the electorate, or there must be some friction to be overcome which will serve to test the depth and force as well as the numerical extent of the feeling behind the new proposal. In the United Kingdom we have one official brake, the House of Lords, and several unofficial ones, the civil service, the permanent determined opposition of the Bench to democratic measures, the Press, and all that we call Society. All these brakes act in one way only. There is no brake upon reaction—a lack which becomes more serious in proportion as the Conservative party acquires a definite and constructive policy of its own. In this situation the Liberal party set itself to deal with the official brake by the simple method of reducing its effective strength, but, to be honest, without having made up its mind as to the nature of the brake which it would like to substitute. On this question a few general remarks would seem to be in place. The function of a check on the House of Commons is to secure reconsideration. Conservative leaders are in the right when they point to the accidental elements that go to the constitution of parliamentary majorities. The programme of any general election is always composite, and a man finds himself compelled, for example, to choose between a Tariff Reformer whose views on education he approves, and a Free Trader whose educational policy he detests. In part this defect might be remedied by the Proportional system to which, whether against the grain or not, Liberals will find themselves driven the more they insist on the genuinely representative character of the House of Commons. But even a Proportional system would not wholly clear the issues before the electorate. The average man gives his vote on the question which he takes to be most important in itself, and which he supposes to be most likely to come up for immediate settlement. But he is always liable to find his expectations defeated, and a Parliament which is in reality elected on one issue may proceed to deal with quite another. The remedy proposed by the Parliament Bill was a two years' delay, which, it was held, would secure full discussion and considerable opportunity for the manifestation of opinion should it be adverse. This proposal had been put to the constituencies twice over, and had been ratified by them if any legislative proposal ever was ratified. It should enable the House of Commons, as the representatives of the people, to decide freely on the permanent constitution of the country. The Bill itself, however, does not lay down the lines of a permanent settlement. For, to begin with, in leaving the constitution of the House of Lords unaltered it provides a one-sided check, operating only on democratic measures which in any case have to run the gauntlet of the permanent officials, the judges, the Press, and Society. For permanent use the brake must be two-sided. Secondly, it is to be feared that the principle of delay would be an insufficient check upon a large and headstrong majority. What is really needed is that the people should have the opportunity of considering a proposal afresh. This could be secured in either of two ways: (1) by allowing the suspensory veto of the Second Chamber to hold a measure over to a new Parliament; (2) by allowing the House of Commons to submit a bill in the form in which it finally leaves the House to a direct popular vote. It is to my mind regrettable that so many Liberals should have closed the door on the Referendum. It is true that there are many measures to which it would be ill suited. For example, measures affecting a particular class or a particular locality would be apt to go by the board. They might command a large and enthusiastic majority among those primarily affected by them, but only receive a languid assent elsewhere, and they might be defeated by a majority beaten up for extraneous purposes among those without first-hand knowledge of the problems with which they are intended to deal. Again, if a referendum were to work at all it would only be in relation to measures of the first class, and only, if the public convenience is to be consulted, on very rare occasions. In all ordinary cases of insuperable difference between the Houses, the government of the day would accept the postponement of the measure till the new Parliament. But there are measures of urgency, measures of fundamental import, above all, measures which cut across the ordinary lines of party, and with which, in consequence, our system is impotent to deal, and on these the direct consultation of the people would be the most suitable method of solution.[13]

What we need, then, is an impartial second chamber distinctly subordinate to the House of Commons, incapable of touching finance and therefore of overthrowing a ministry, but able to secure the submission of a measure either to the direct vote of the people or to the verdict of a second election—the government of the day having the choice between the alternatives. Such a chamber might be instituted by direct popular election. But the multiplication of elections is not good for the working of democracy, and it would be difficult to reconcile a directly elected house to a subordinate position. It might, therefore, as an alternative, be elected on a proportional system by the House of Commons itself, its members retaining their seat for two Parliaments. To bridge over the change half of the chamber for the present Parliament might be elected by the existing House of Lords, and their representatives retiring at the end of this Parliament would leave the next House of Commons and every future House of Commons with one-half of the chamber to elect. This Second Chamber would then reflect in equal proportions the existing and the last House of Commons, and the balance between parties should be fairly held.[14] This chamber would have ample power of securing reasonable amendments and would also have good ground for exercising moderation in pressing its views. If the public were behind the measure it would know that in the end the House of Commons could carry it in its teeth, whether by referendum or by a renewed vote of confidence at a general election. The Commons, on their side, would have reasons for exhibiting a conciliatory temper. They would not wish to be forced either to postpone or to appeal. As to which method they would choose they would have absolute discretion, and if they went to the country with a series of popular measures hung up and awaiting their return for ratification, they would justly feel themselves in a strong position.

So far as to forms. The actual future of democracy, however, rests upon deeper issues. It is bound up with the general advance of civilization. The organic character of society is, we have seen, in one sense, an ideal. In another sense it is an actuality. That is to say, nothing of any import affects the social life on one side without setting up reactions all through the tissue. Hence, for example, we cannot maintain great political progress without some

---

[13] I need hardly add that financial measures are entirely unsuited to a referendum. Financial and executive control go together, and to take either of them out of the hands of the majority in the House of Commons is not to reform our system but to destroy it root and branch. The same is not true of legislative control. There are cases in which a government might fairly submit a legislative measure to the people without electing to stand or fall by it.

[14] Probably the best alternative to these proposals is that of a small directly elected Second Chamber, with a provision for a joint session in case of insuperable disagreement, but with no provision for delay. This proposal has the advantage, apparently, of commanding a measure of Conservative support.

corresponding advance on other sides. People are not fully free in their political capacity when they are subject industrially to conditions which take the life and heart out of them. A nation as a whole cannot be in the full sense free while it fears another or gives cause of fear to another. The social problem must be viewed as a whole. We touch here the greatest weakness in modern reform movements. The spirit of specialism has invaded political and social activity, and in greater and greater degree men consecrate their whole energy to a particular cause to the almost cynical disregard of all other considerations. "Not such the help, nor these the defenders" which this moment of the world's progress needs. Rather we want to learn our supreme lesson from the school of Cobden. For them the political problem was one, manifold in its ramifications but undivided in its essence. It was a problem of realizing liberty. We have seen reason to think that their conception of liberty was too thin, and that to appreciate its concrete content we must understand it as resting upon mutual restraint and value it as a basis of mutual aid. For us, therefore, harmony serves better as a unifying conception. It remains for us to carry it through with the same logical cogency, the same practical resourcefulness, the same driving force that inspired the earlier Radicals, that gave fire to Cobden's statistics, and lent compelling power to the eloquence of Bright. We need less of the fanatics of sectarianism and more of the unifying mind. Our reformers must learn to rely less on the advertising value of immediate success and more on the deeper but less striking changes of practice or of feeling, to think less of catching votes and more of convincing opinion. We need a fuller co-operation among those of genuine democratic feeling and more agreement as to the order of reform. At present progress is blocked by the very competition of many causes for the first place in the advance. Here, again, devolution will help us, but what would help still more would be a clearer sense of the necessity of co-operation between all who profess and call themselves democrats, based on a fuller appreciation of the breadth and the depth of their own meaning. The advice seems cold to the fiery spirits, but they may come to learn that the vision of justice in the wholeness of her beauty kindles a passion that may not flare up into moments of dramatic scintillation, but burns with the enduring glow of the central heat.

BIBLIOGRAPHY

LOCKE.—Second Treatise on Civil Government (1689).
PAINE.—The Rights of Man (1792).
BENTHAM.—Principles of Morals and Legislation (1789!).
J. S. MILL.—Principles of Political Economy (Books IV and V).
On Liberty.
Representative Government.
The Subjection of Women.
Autobiography.
COBDEN.—Political Writings.
BRIGHT.—Speeches.
MAZZINI.—The Duties of Man.
Thoughts on Democracy in Europe.
JEVONS.—The State in Relation to Labour.
T. H. GREEN.—Principles of Political Obligation.
Liberal Legislation and Freedom of Contract (*Works*, vol. iii).
MORLEY.—Life of Cobden.
Life of Gladstone.
F. W. HIRST.—The Manchester School.
G. LOWES DICKINSON.—Liberty and Justice.
PROF. H. JONES.—The Working Faith of the Social Reformer.
PROF. McCUNN.—Six Radical Thinkers.

Echo Library
www.echo-library.com

Echo Library uses advanced digital print-on-demand technology to build and preserve an exciting world class collection of rare and out-of-print books, making them readily available for everyone to enjoy.

Situated just yards from Teddington Lock on the River Thames, Echo Library was founded in 2005 by Tom Cherrington, a specialist dealer in rare and antiquarian books with a passion for literature.

Please visit our website for a complete catalogue of our books, which includes foreign language titles.

The Right to Read
Echo Library actively supports the Royal National Institute of the Blind's Right to Read initiative by publishing a comprehensive range of large print and clear print titles.

Large Print titles are in 16 point Tiresias font as recommended by the RNIB.

Clear Print titles are in 13 point Tiresias font and designed for those who find standard print difficult to read.

Customer Service
If there is a serious error in the text or layout please send details to feedback@echo-library.com and we will supply a corrected copy. If there is a printing fault or the book is damaged please refer to your supplier.